Voyages in Steampunk

Episode 2

This book belongs to:

____

Cracked Palette Designs L.L.C.
Kindle Direct Publishing
Voyages in Steampunk
Episode 2

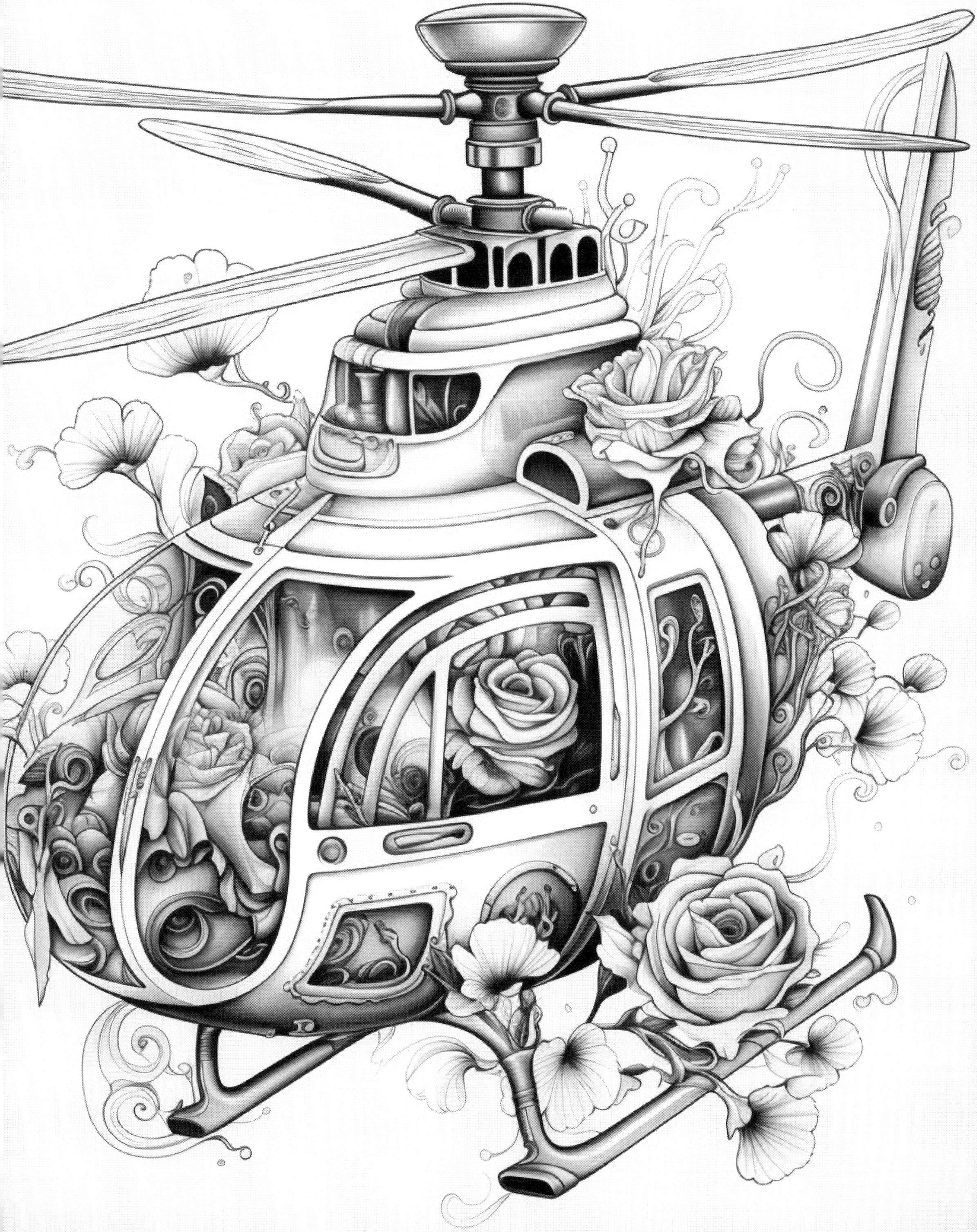

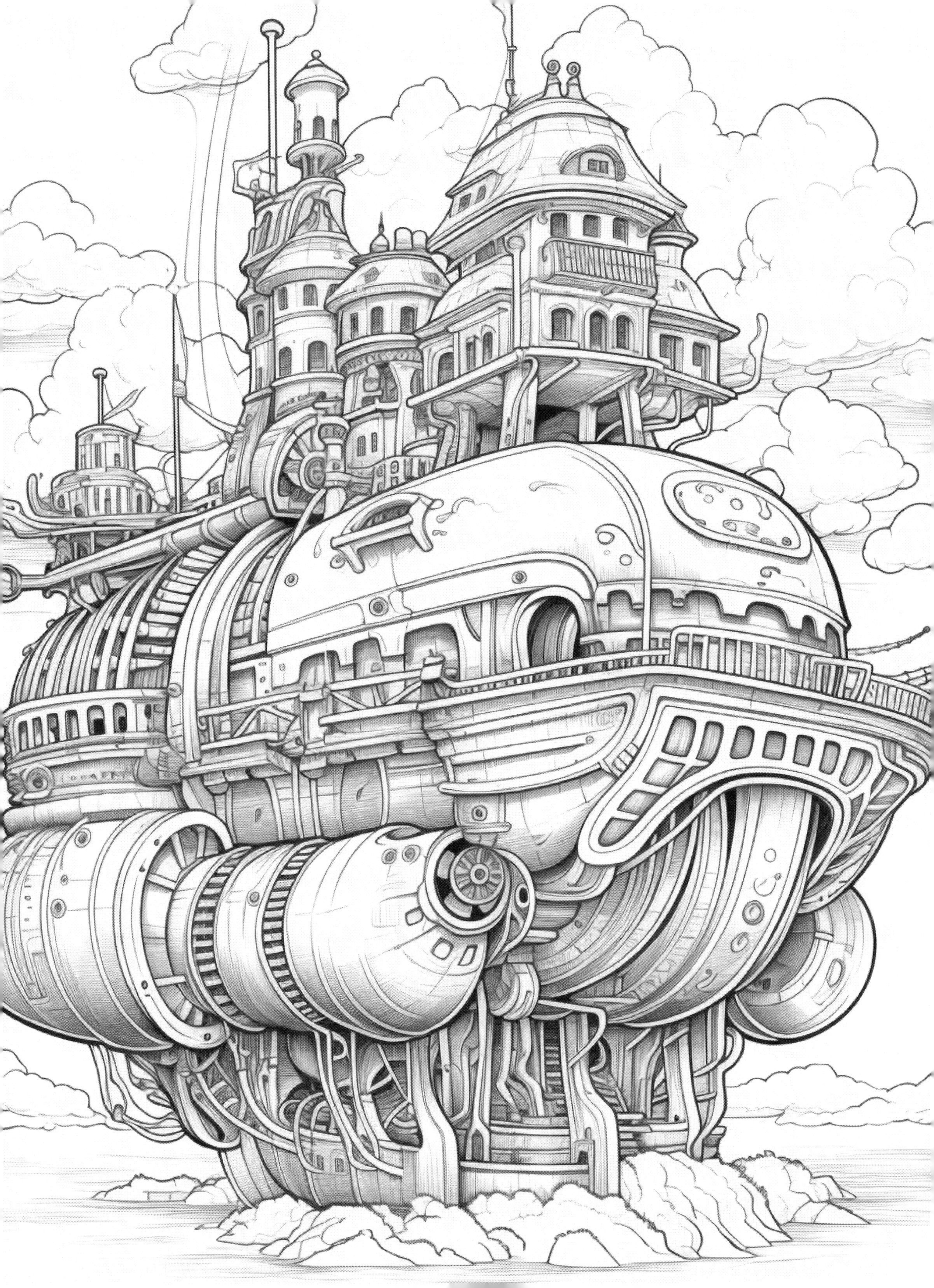

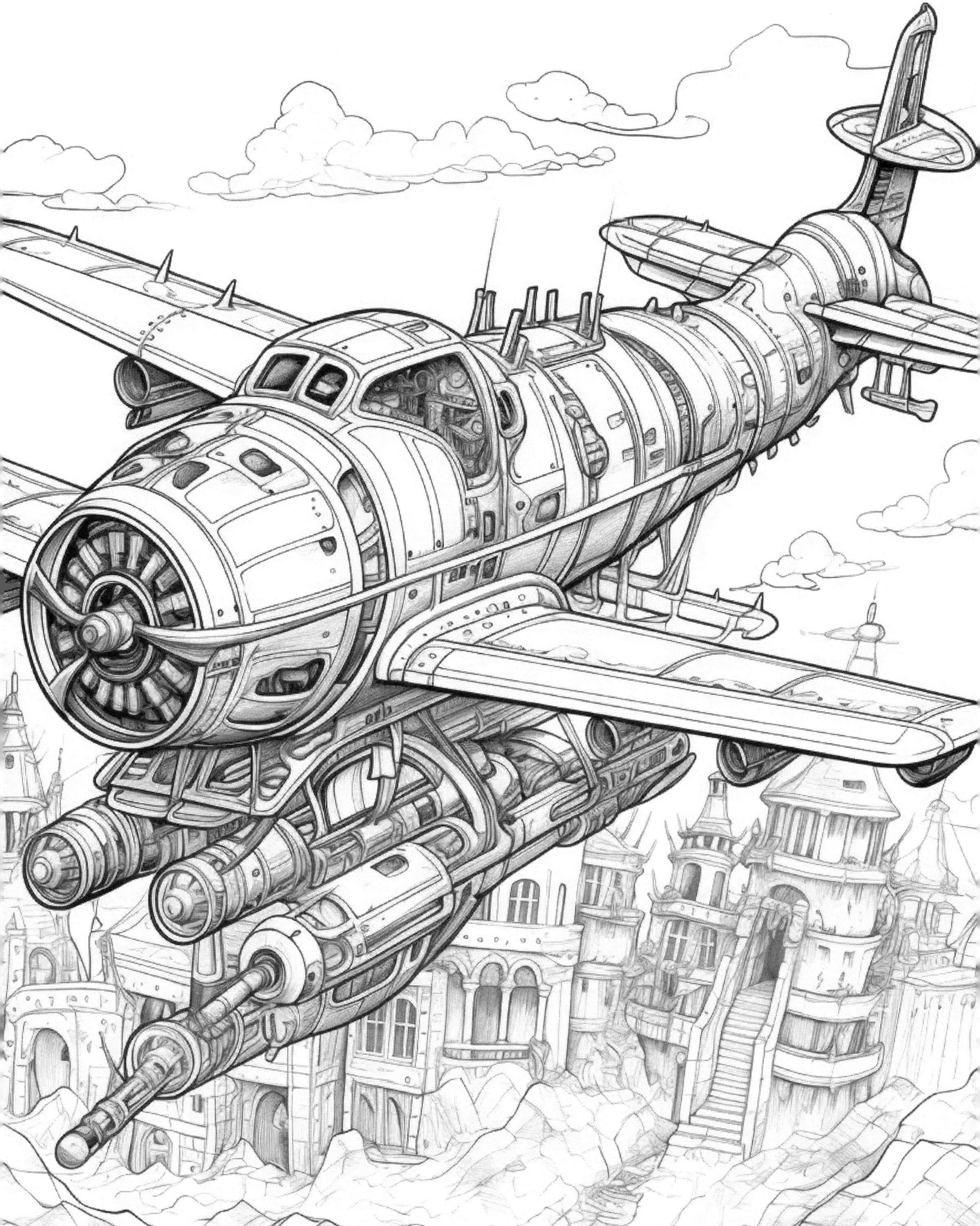

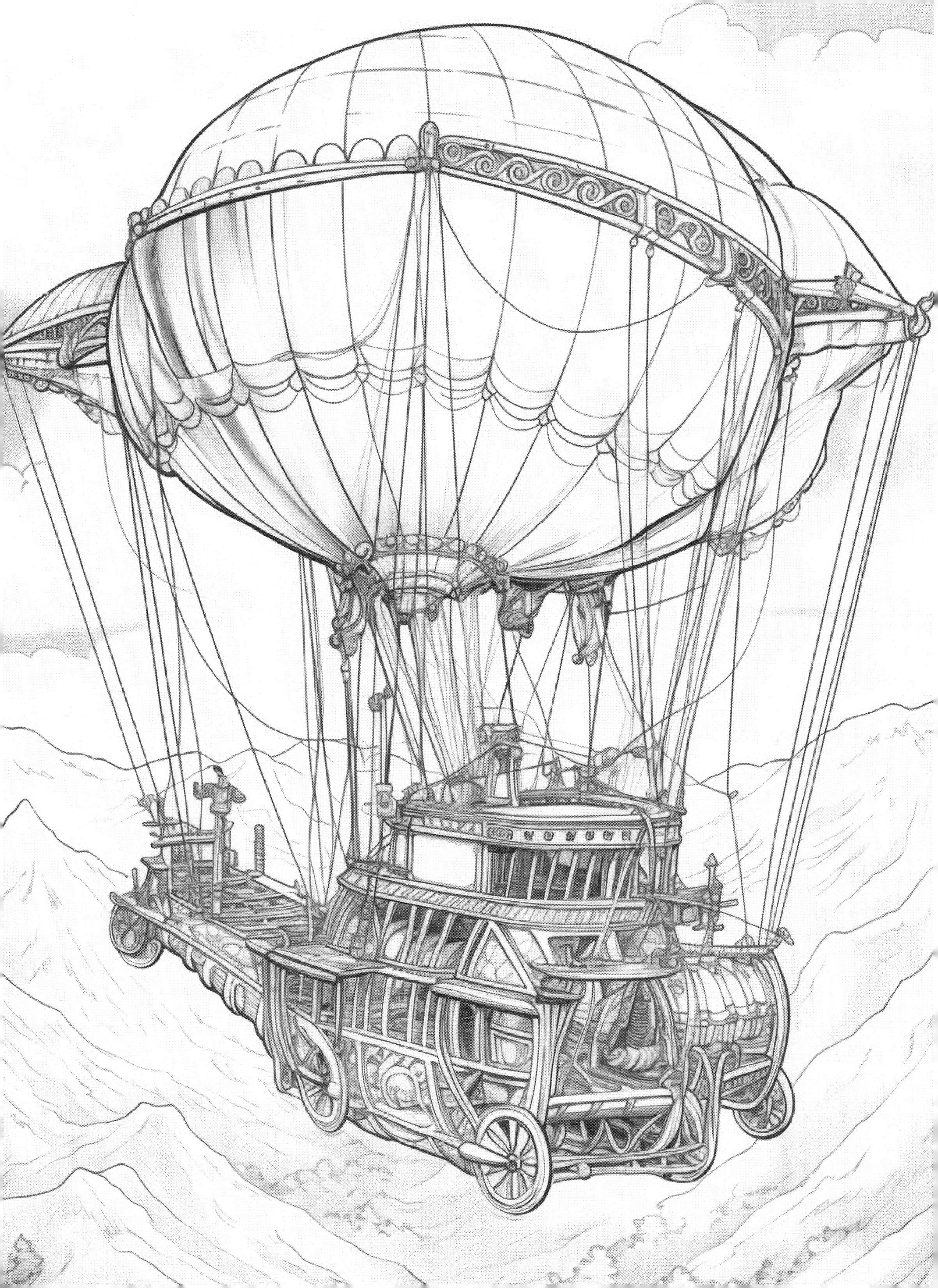

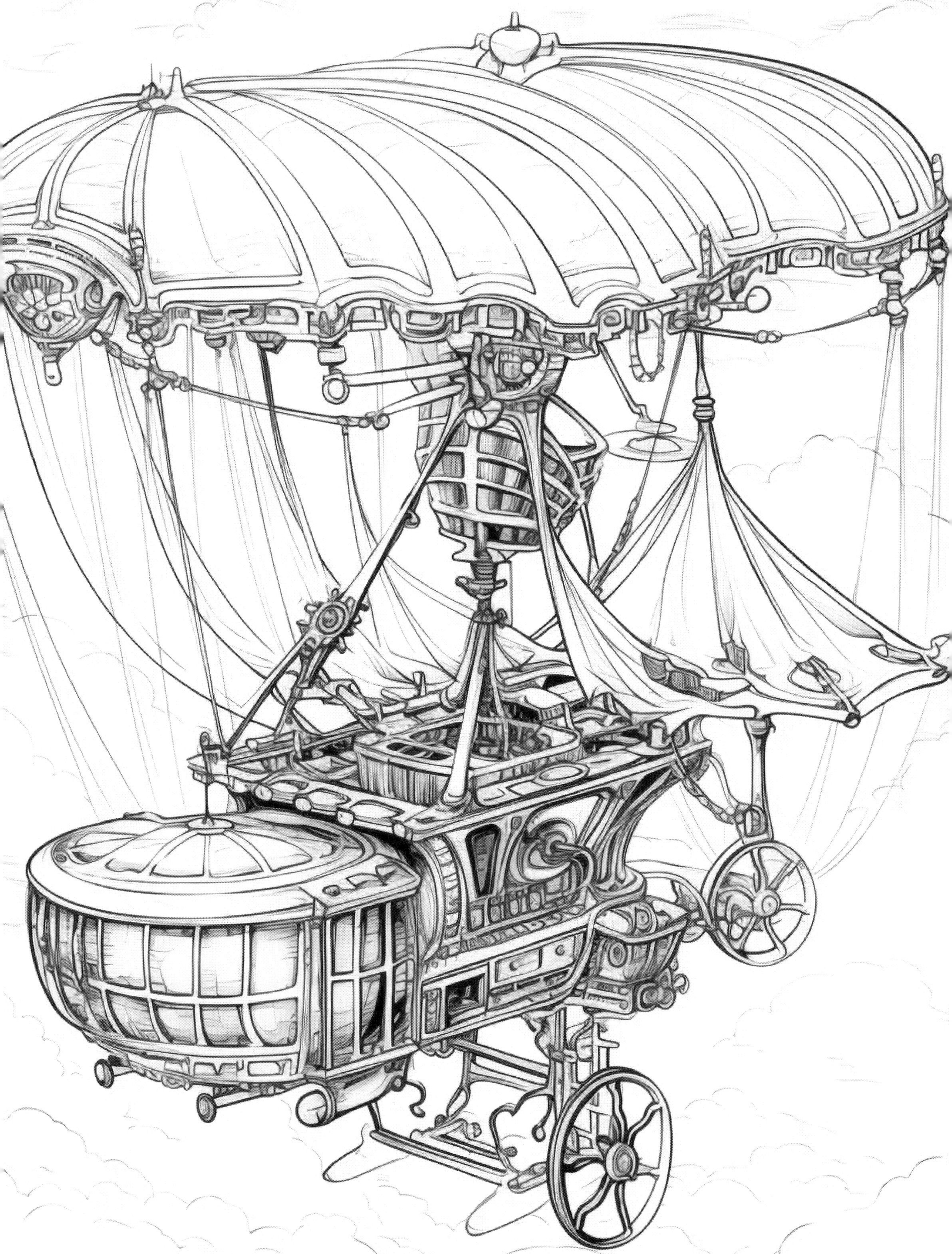

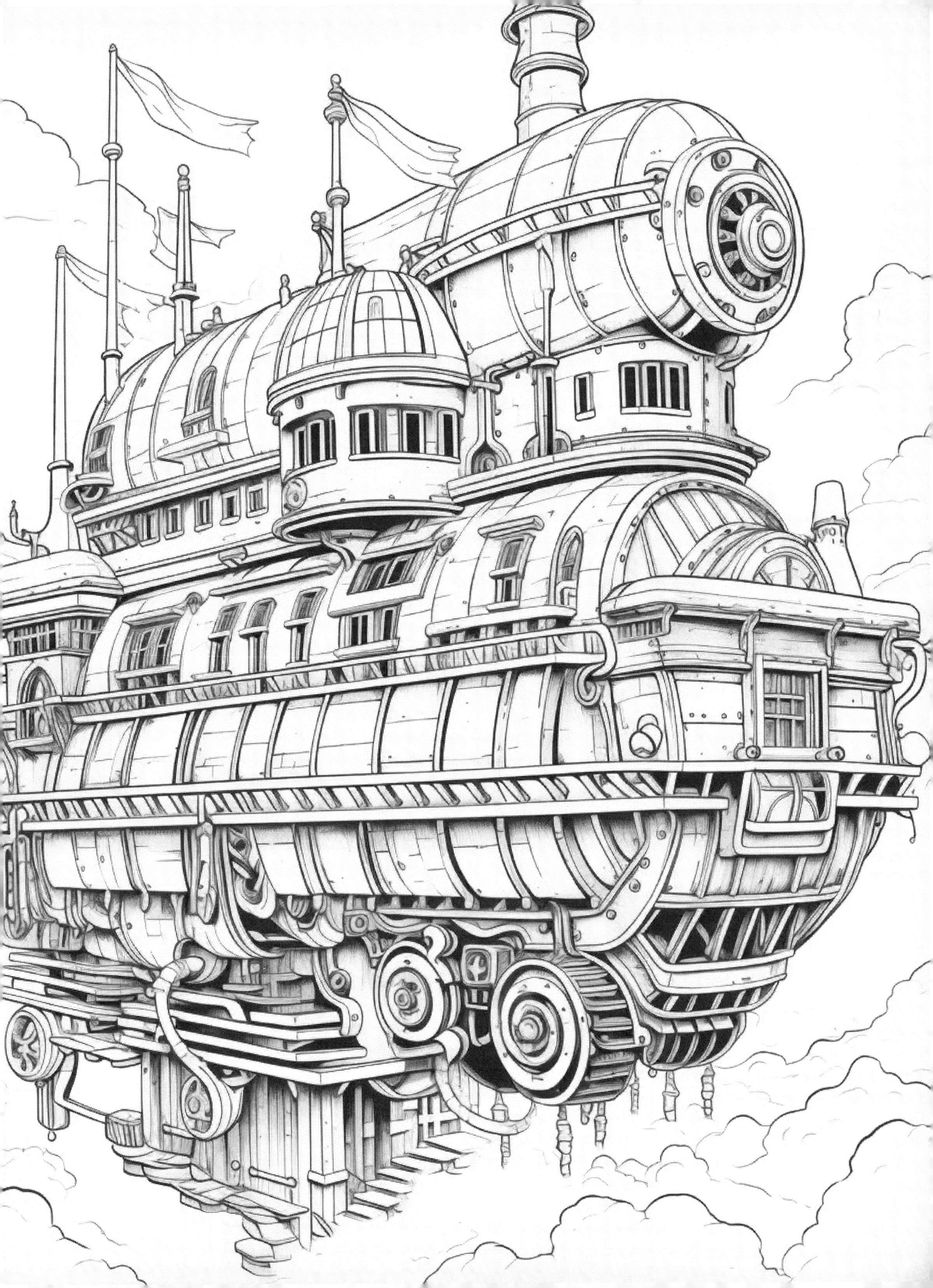

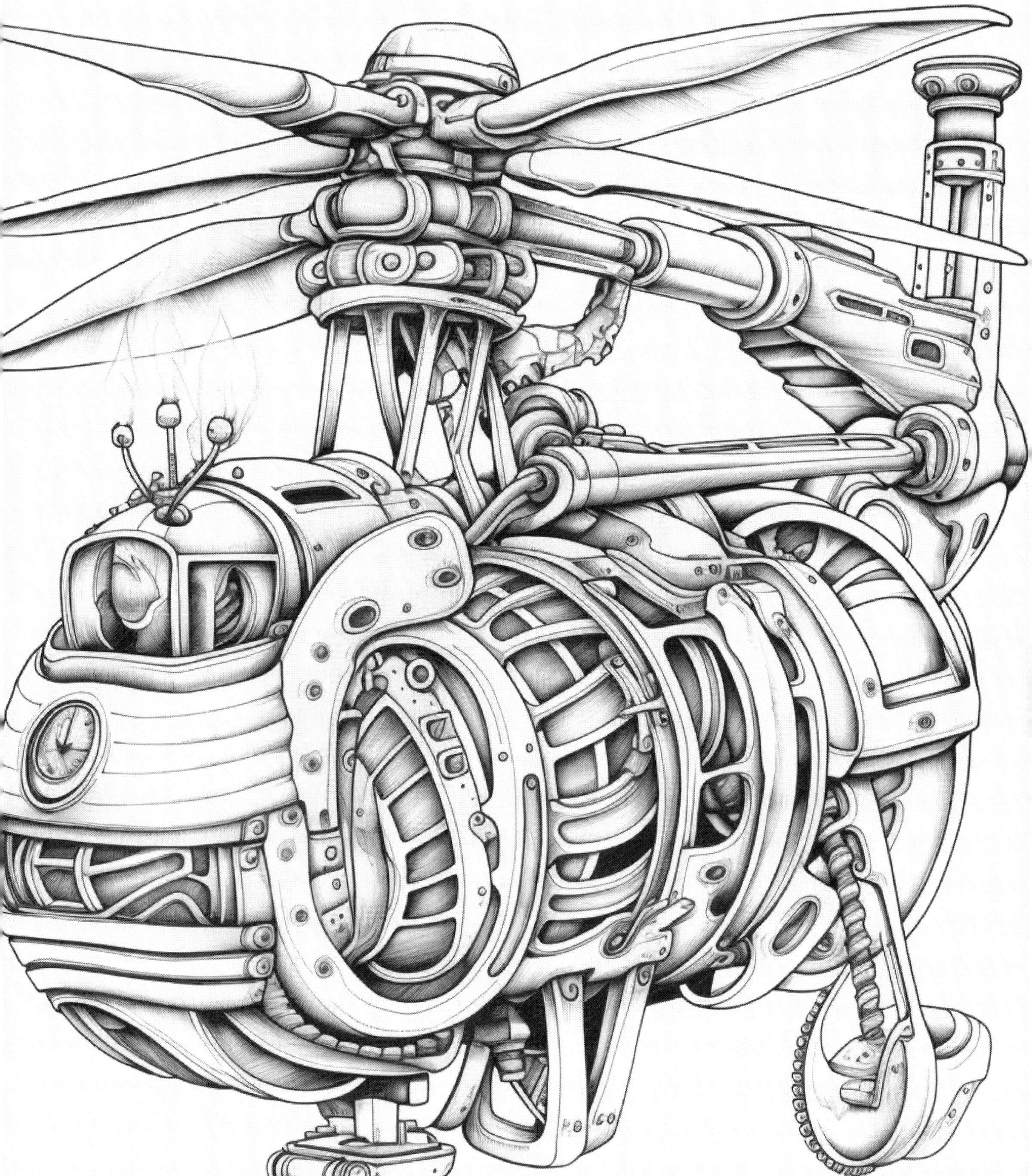

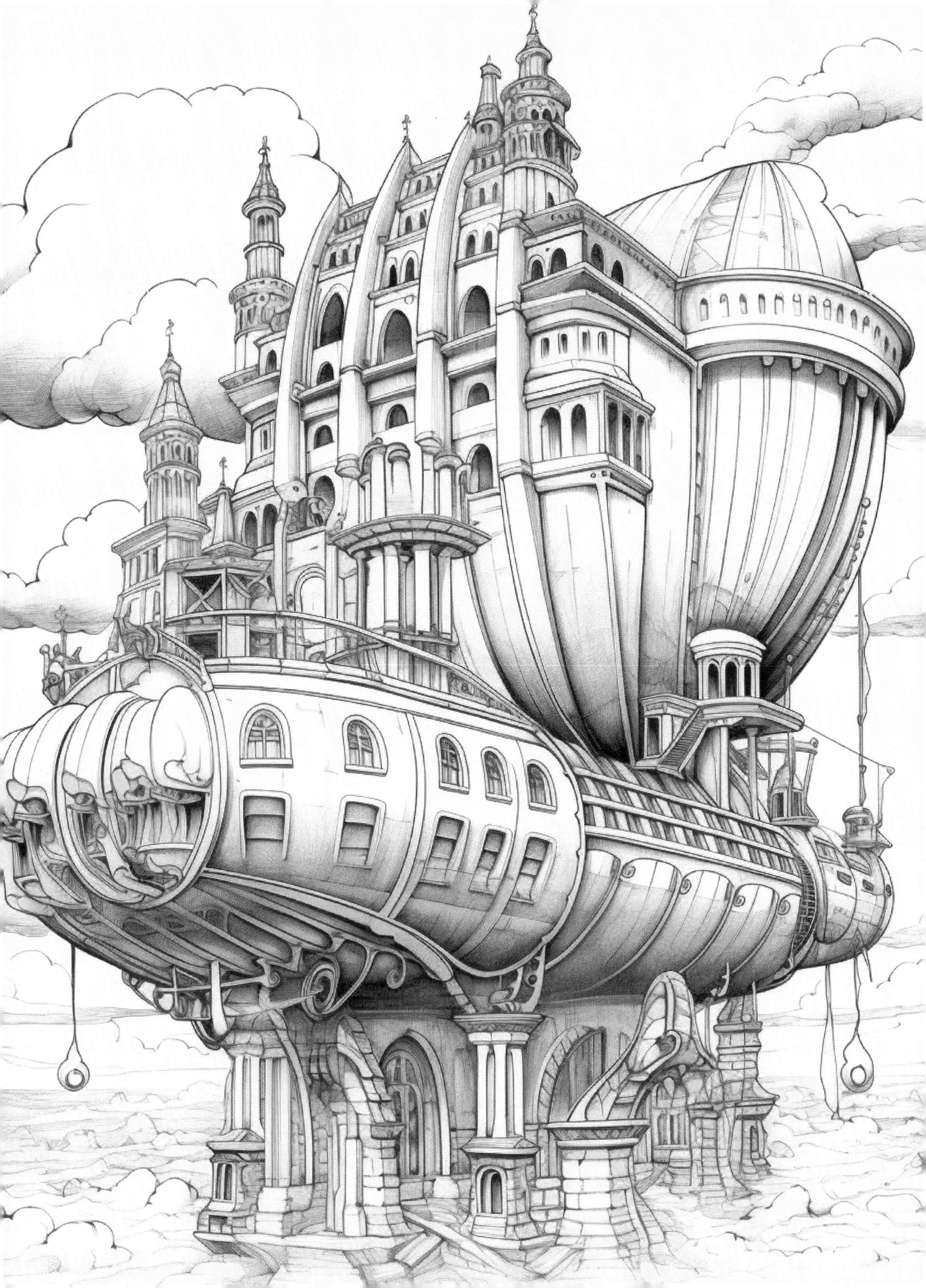

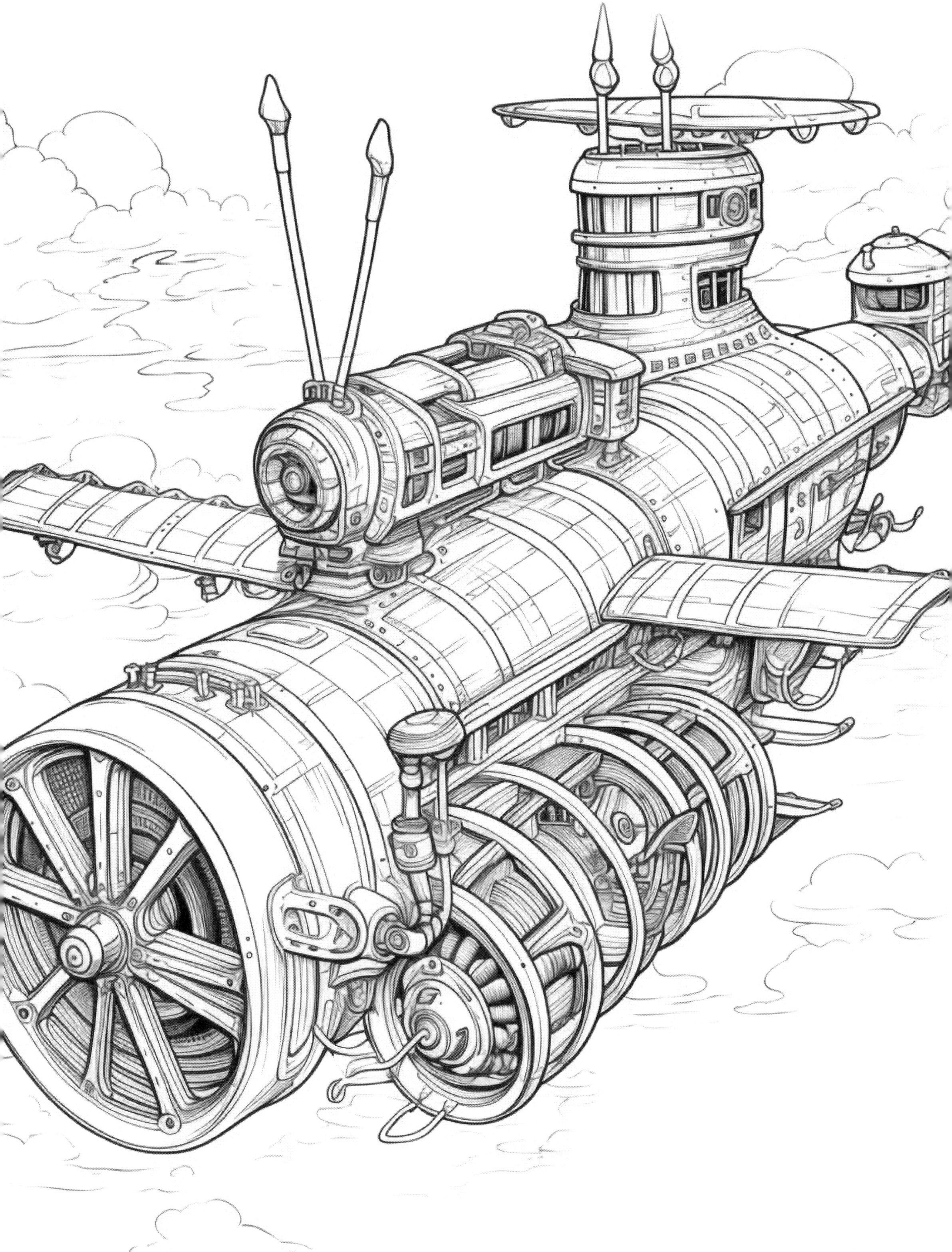

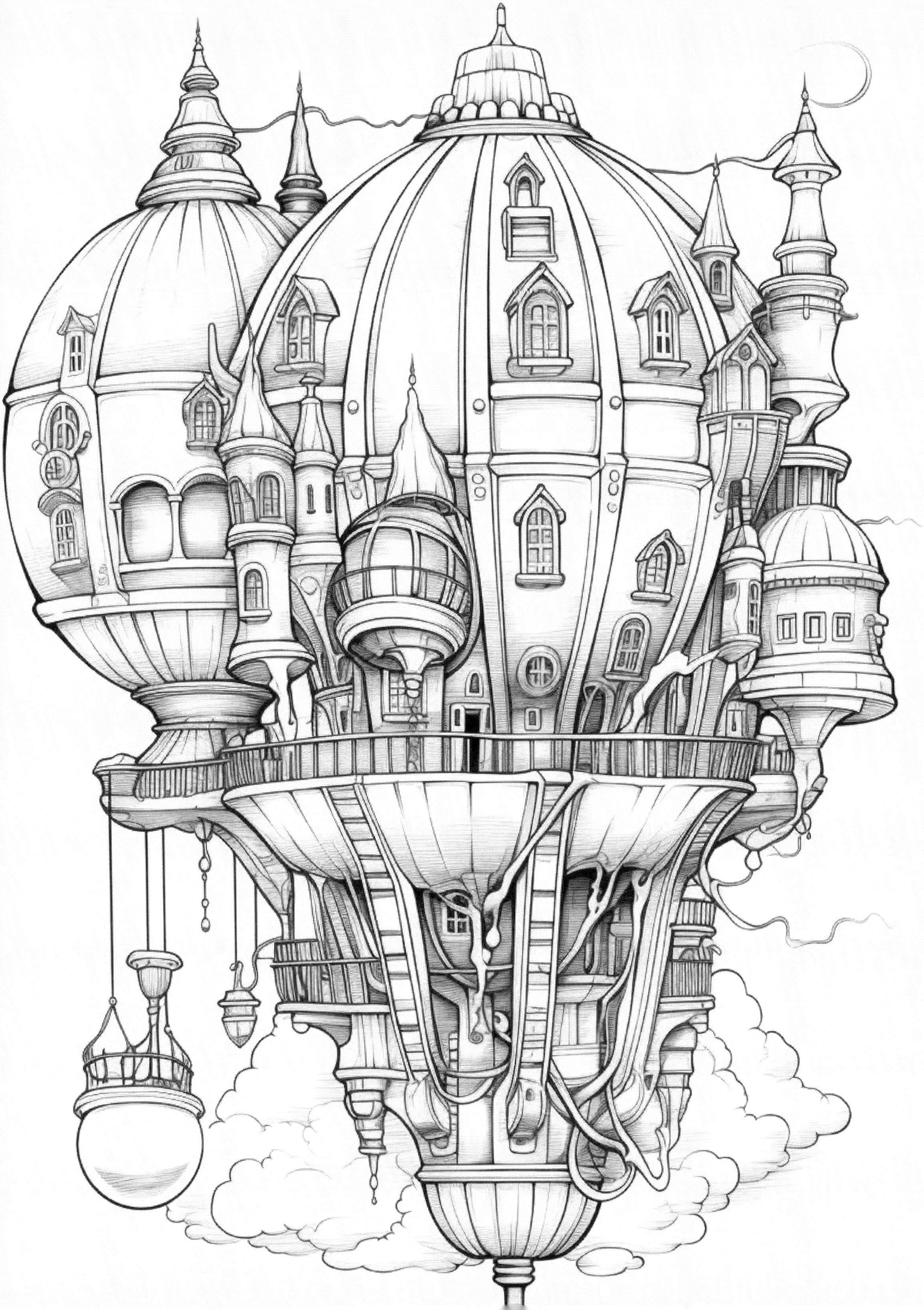

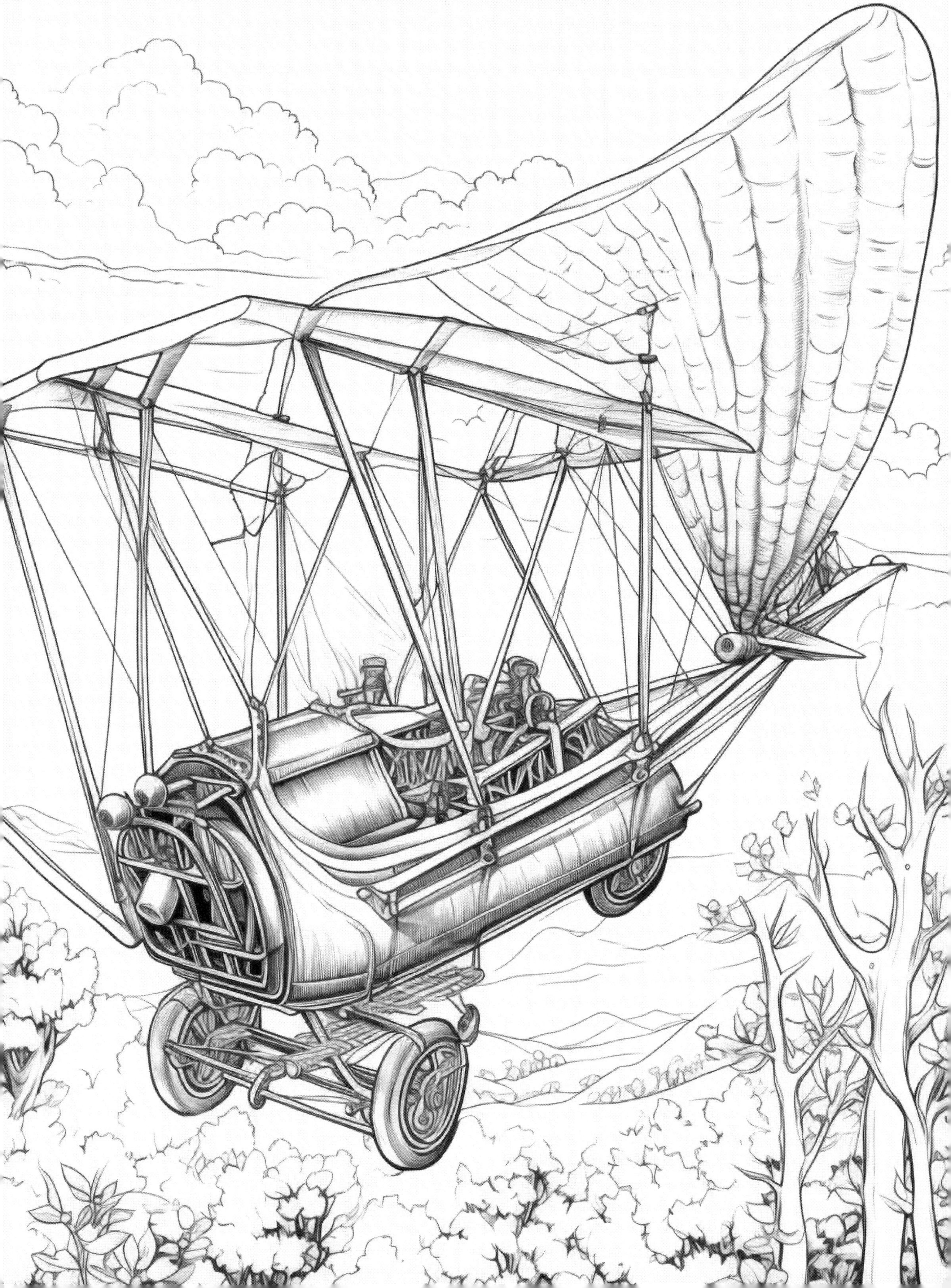

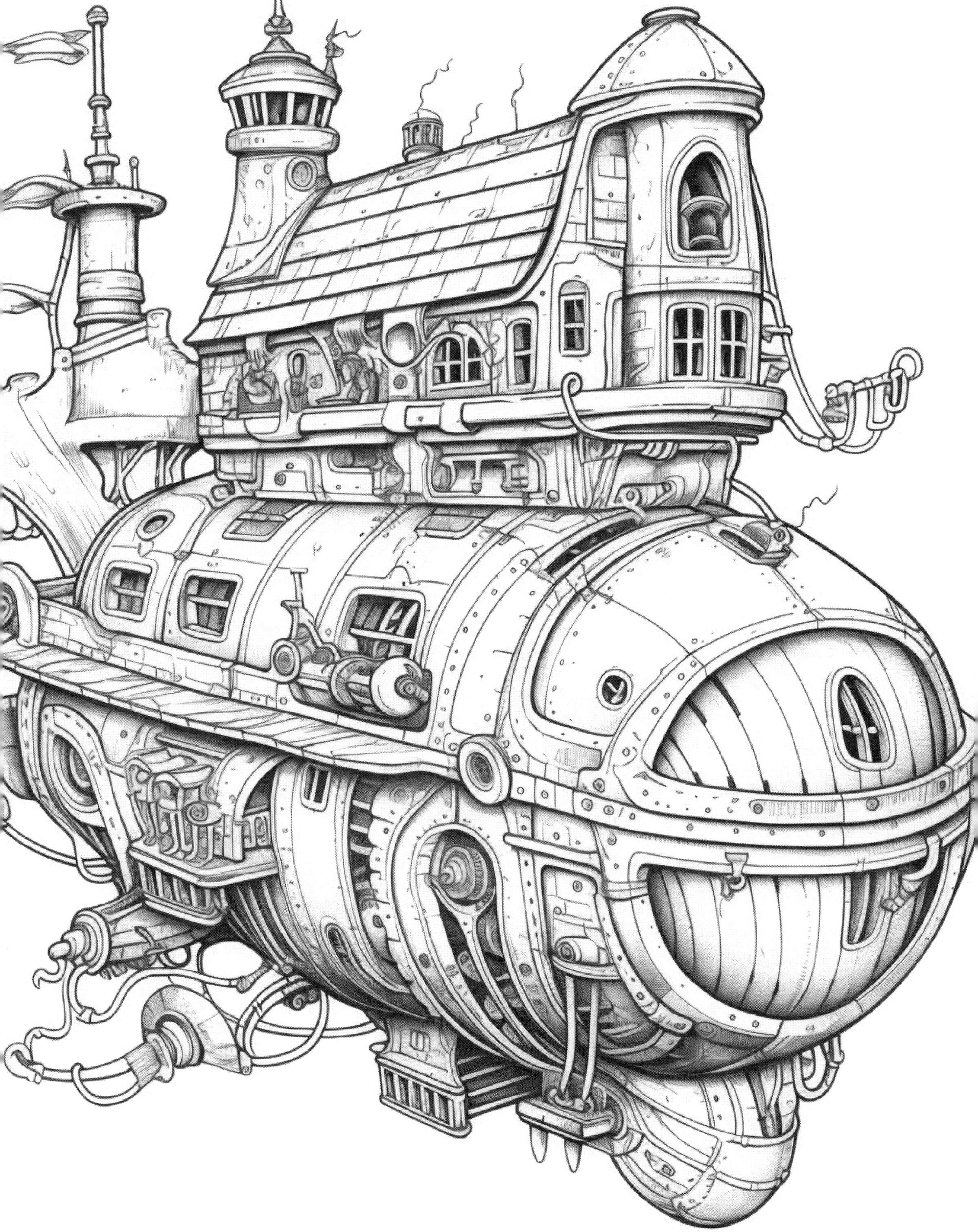

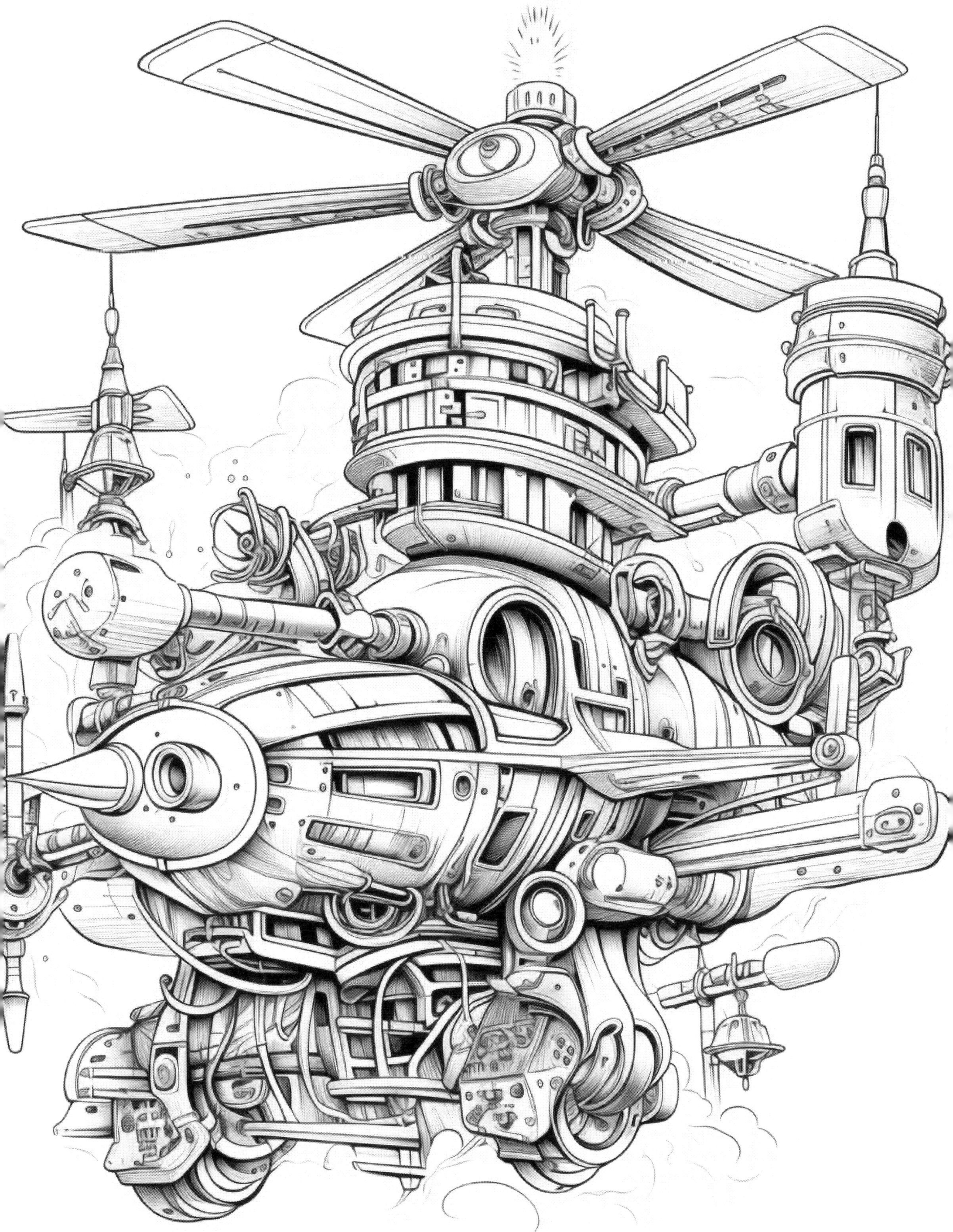

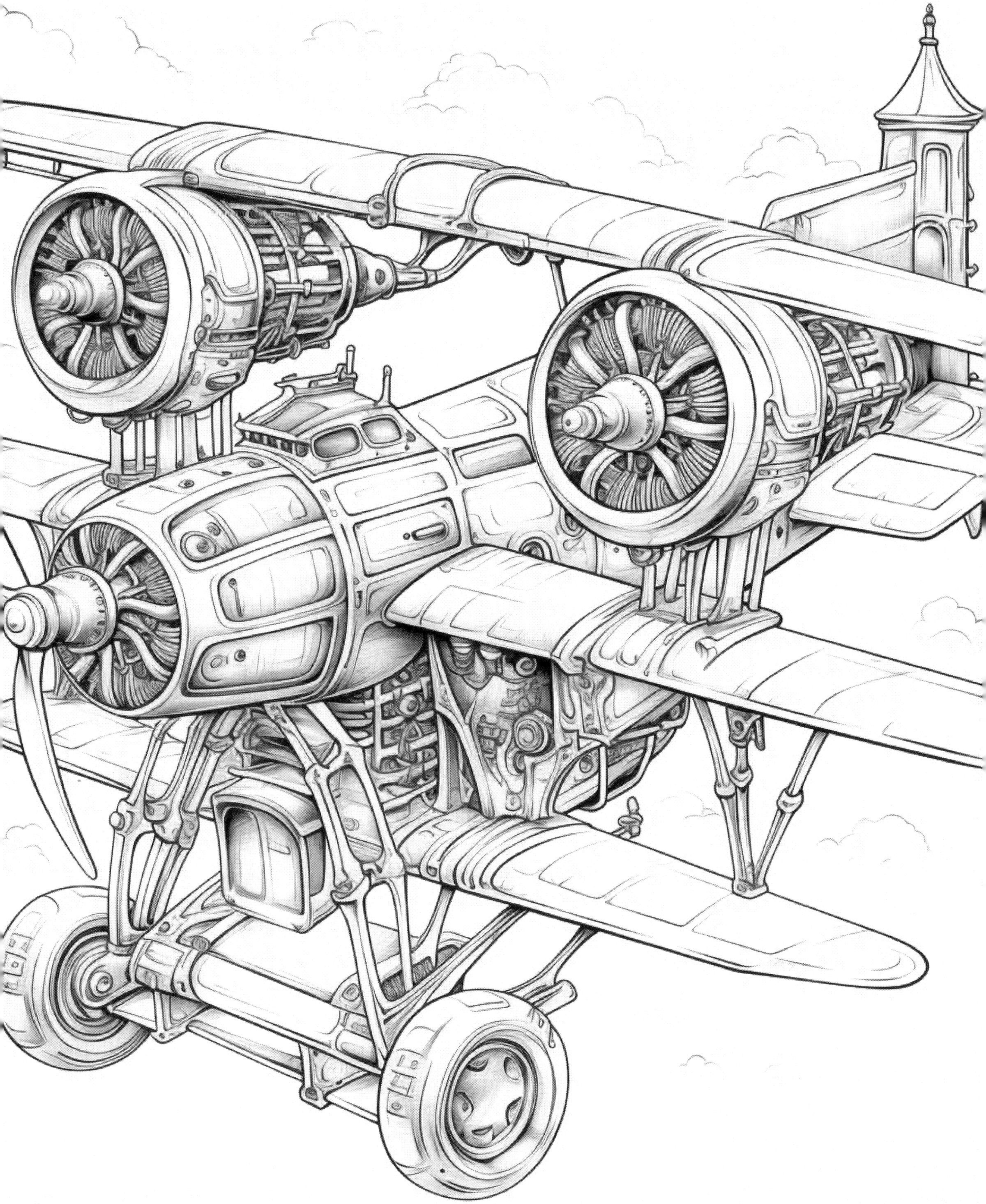

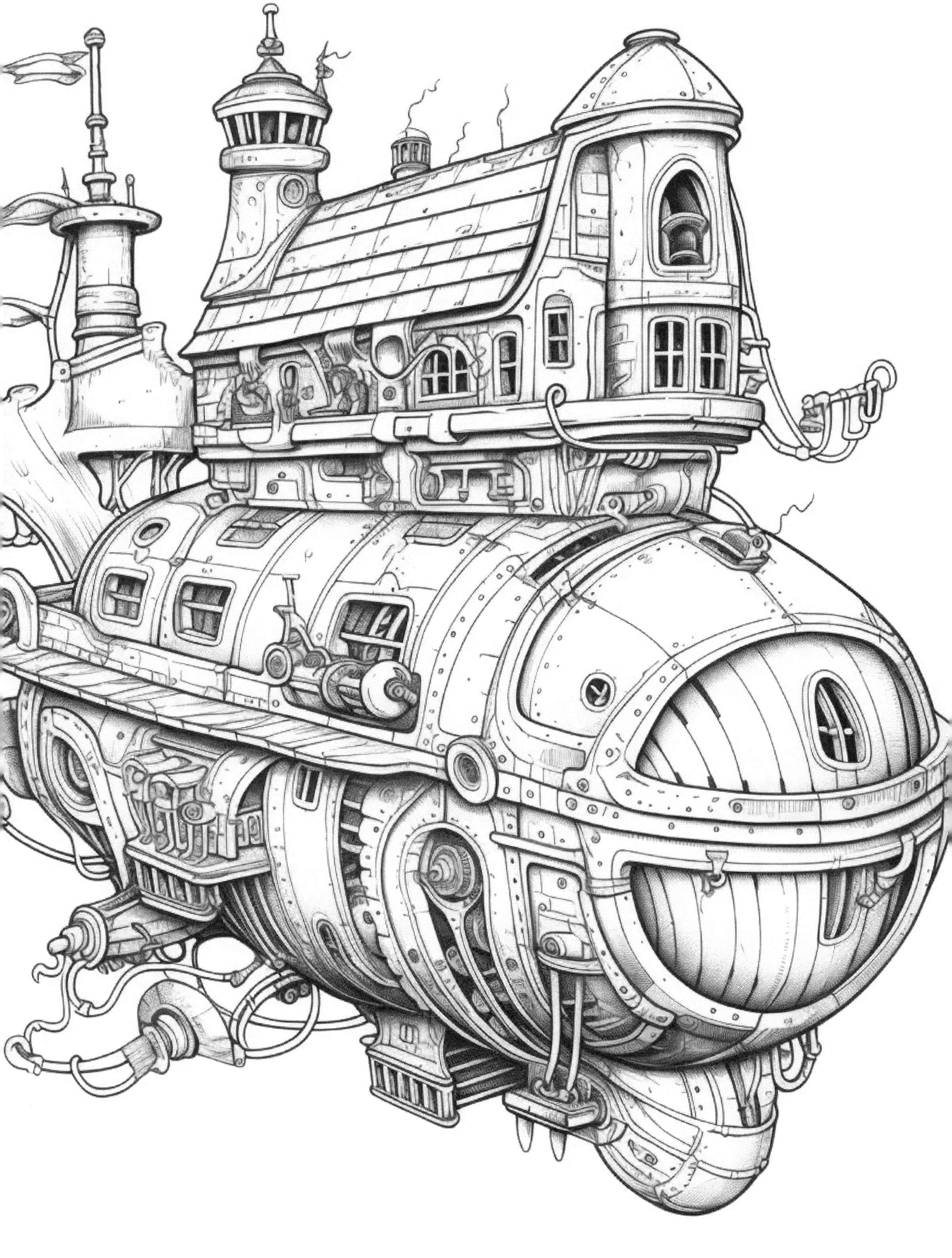

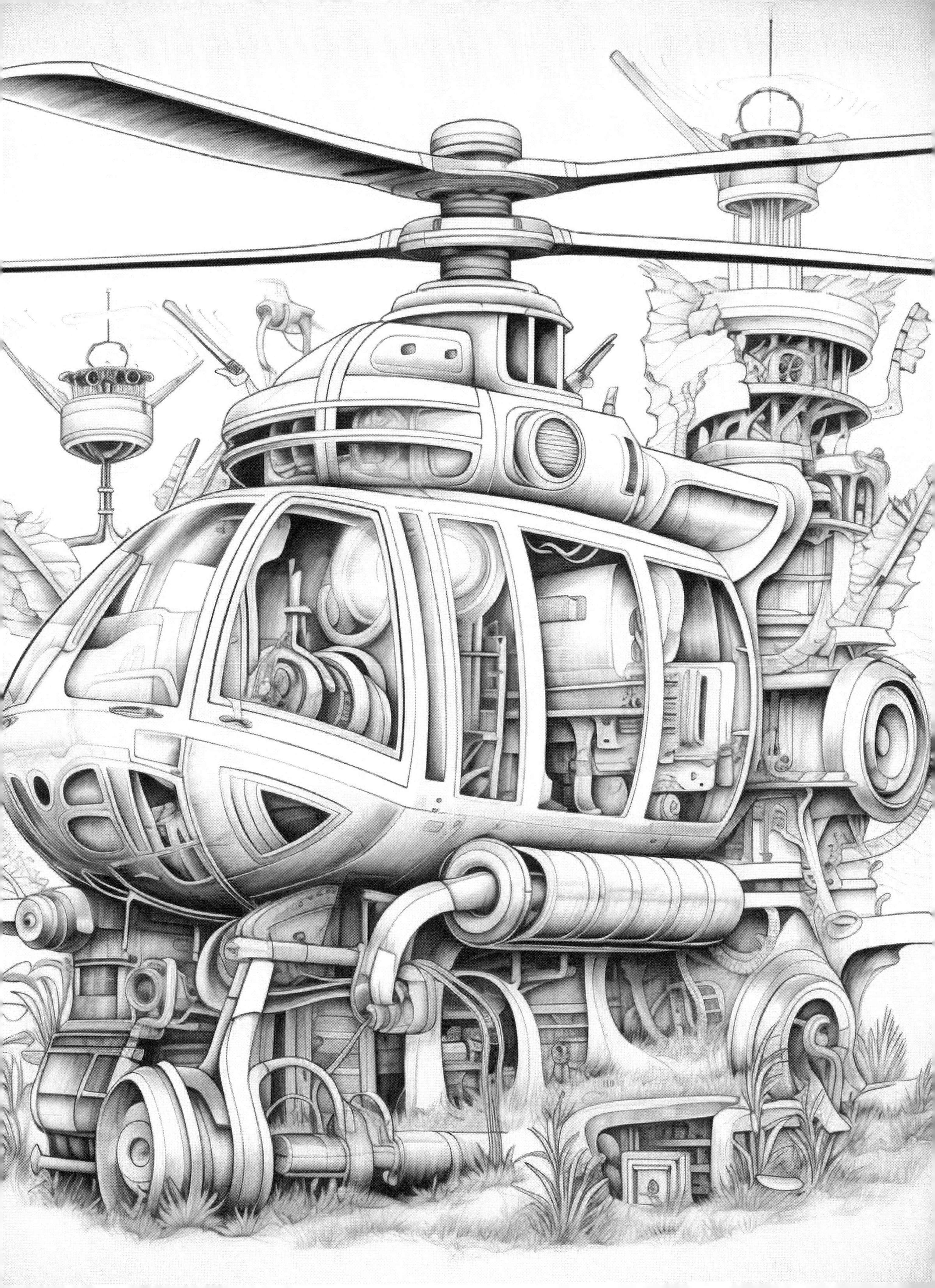

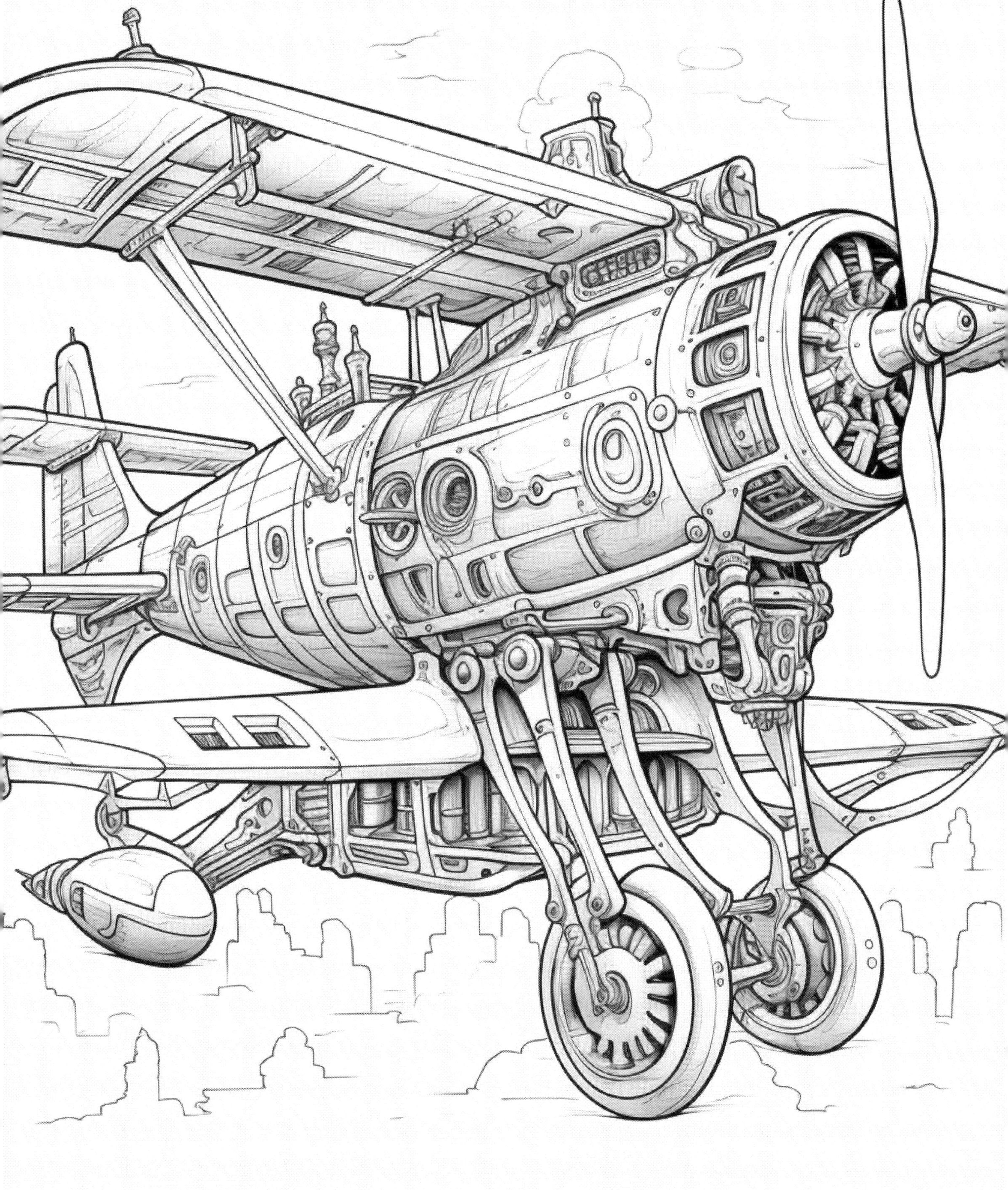

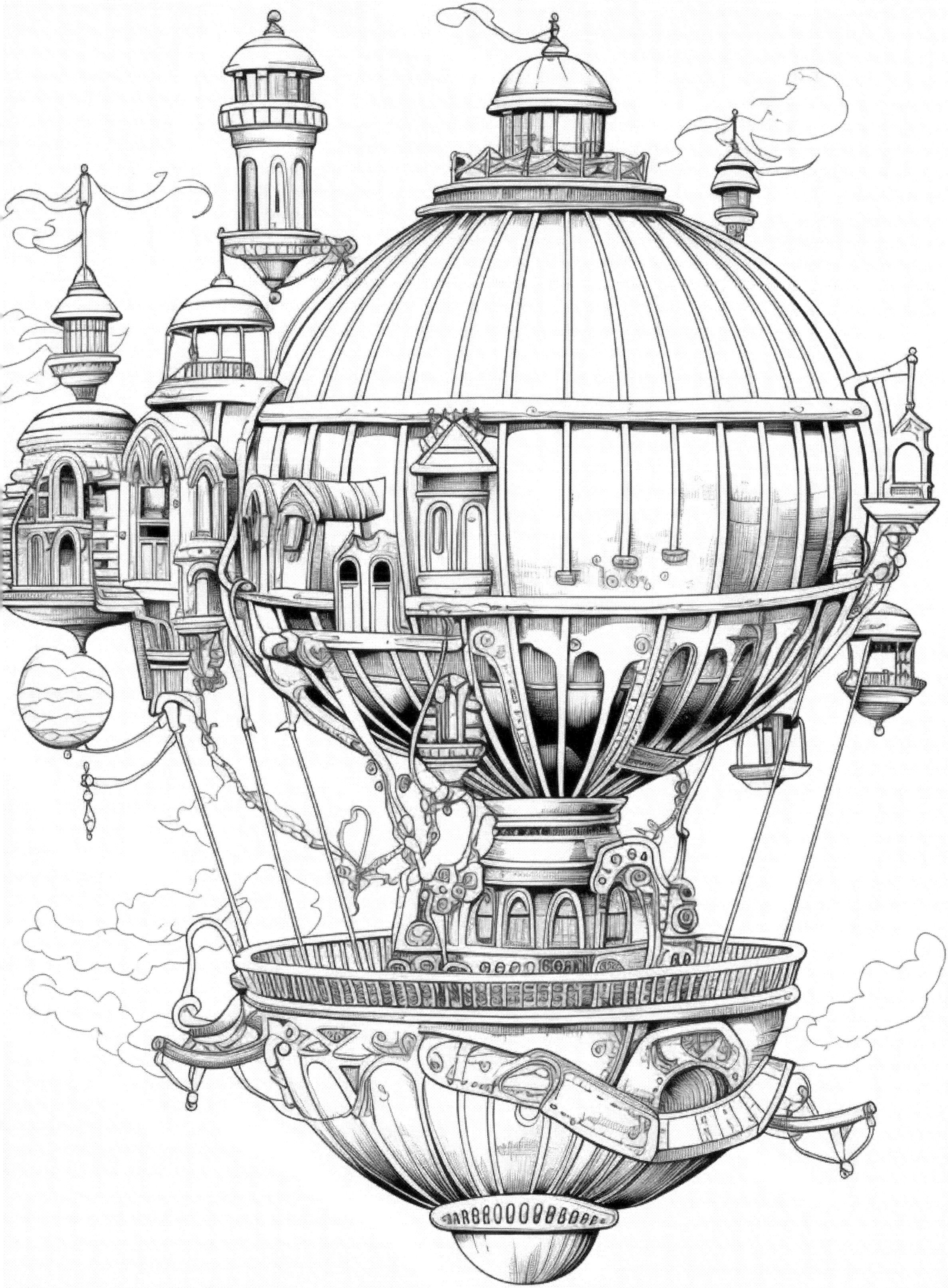

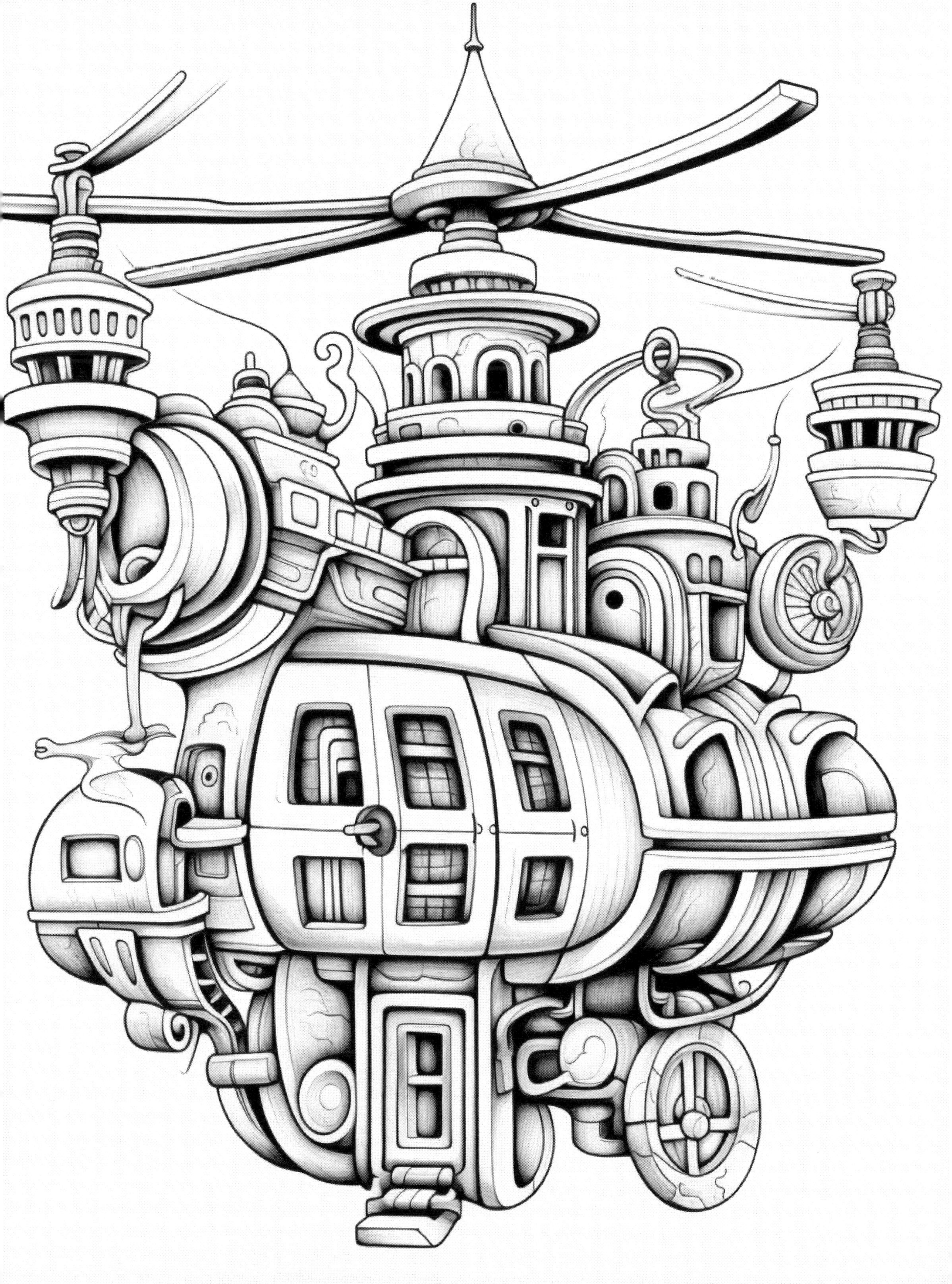

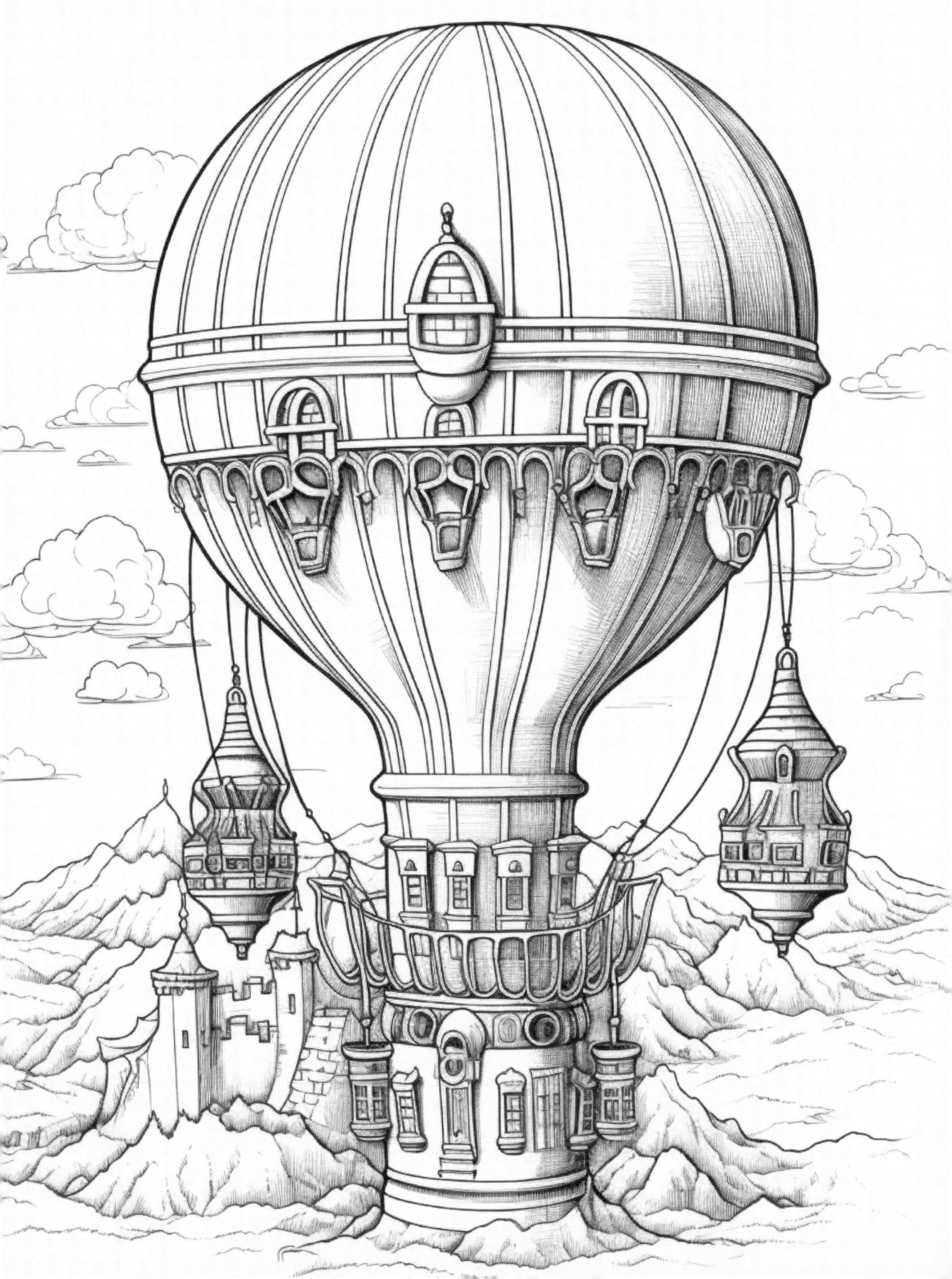

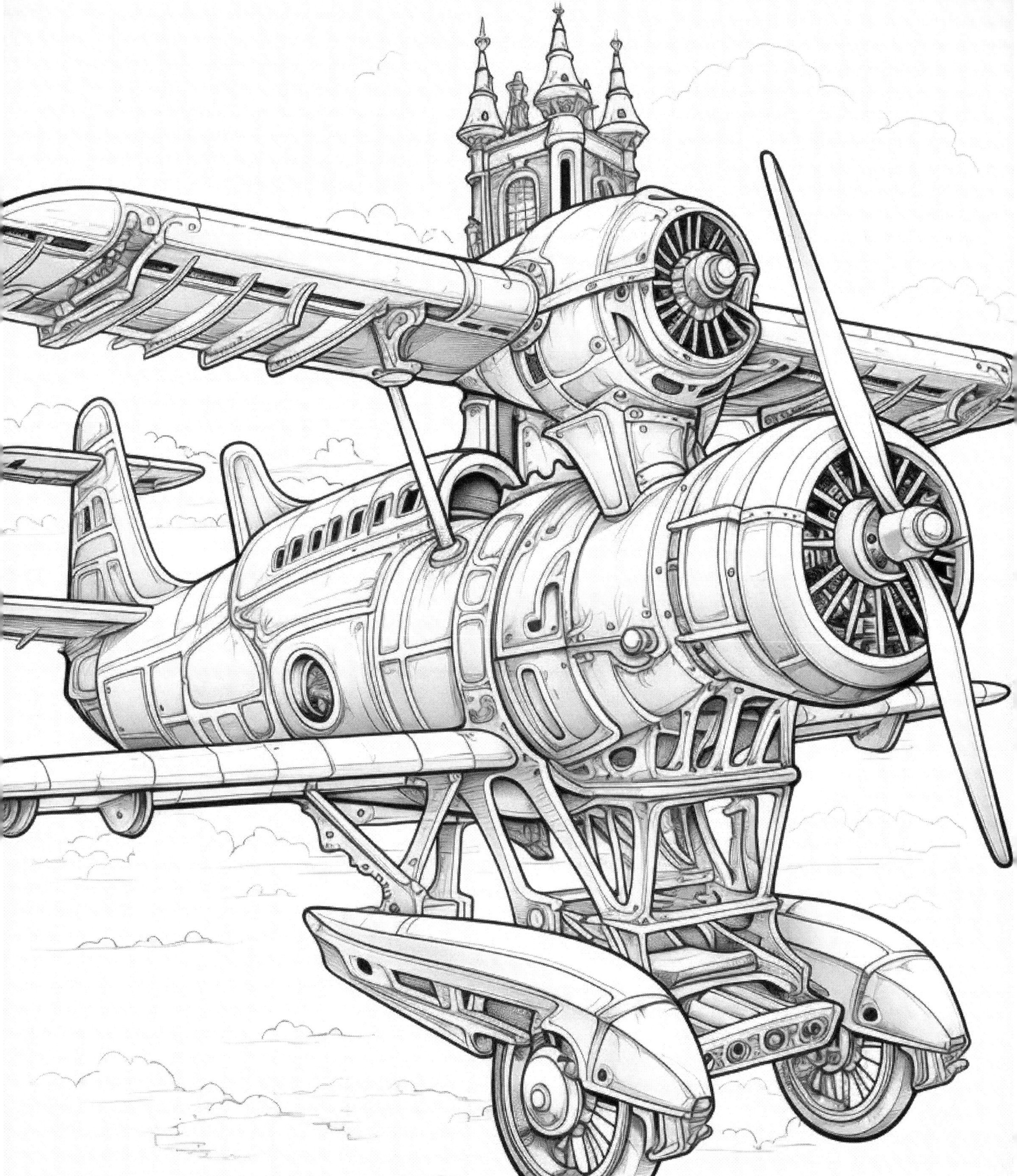

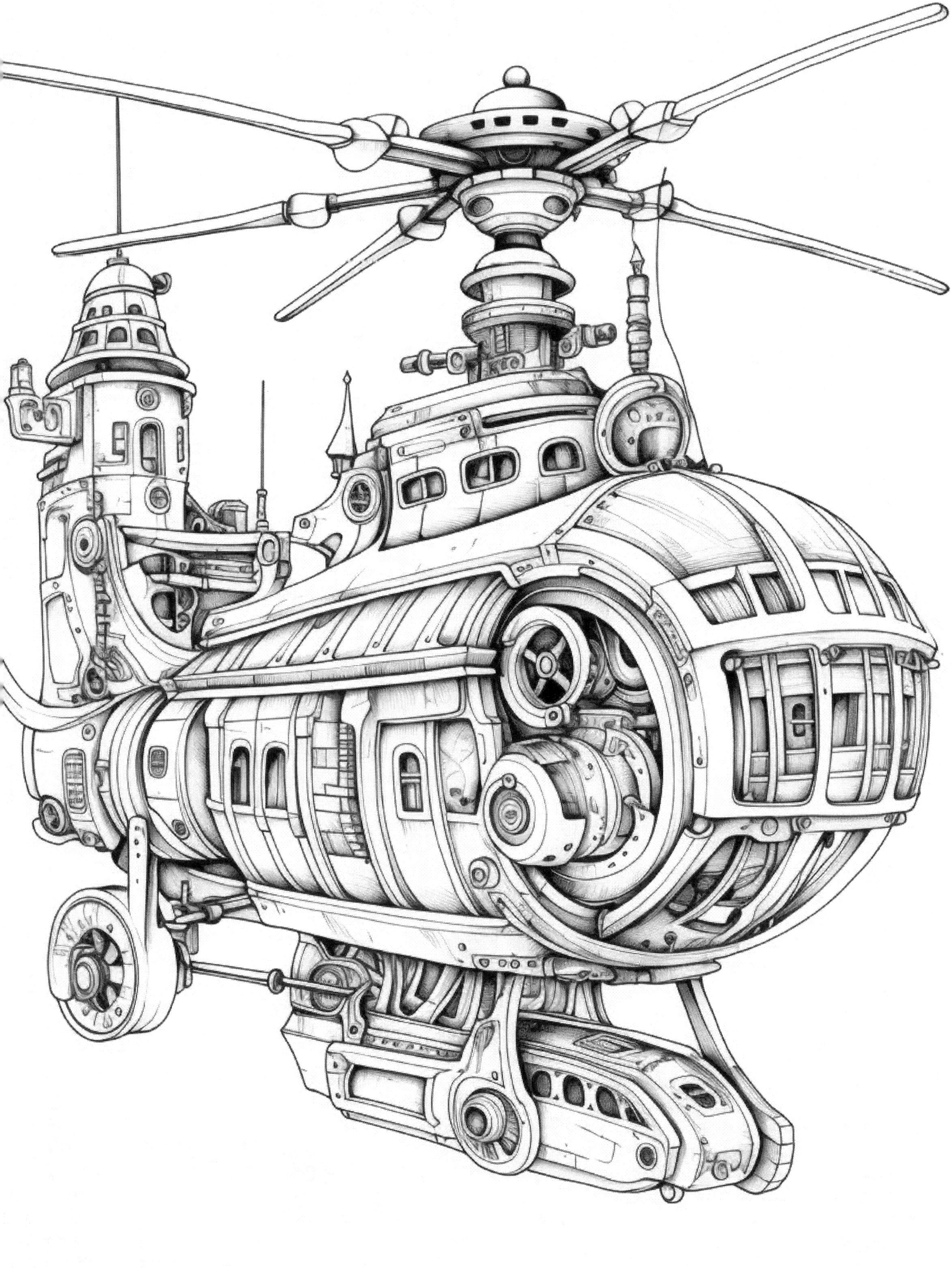

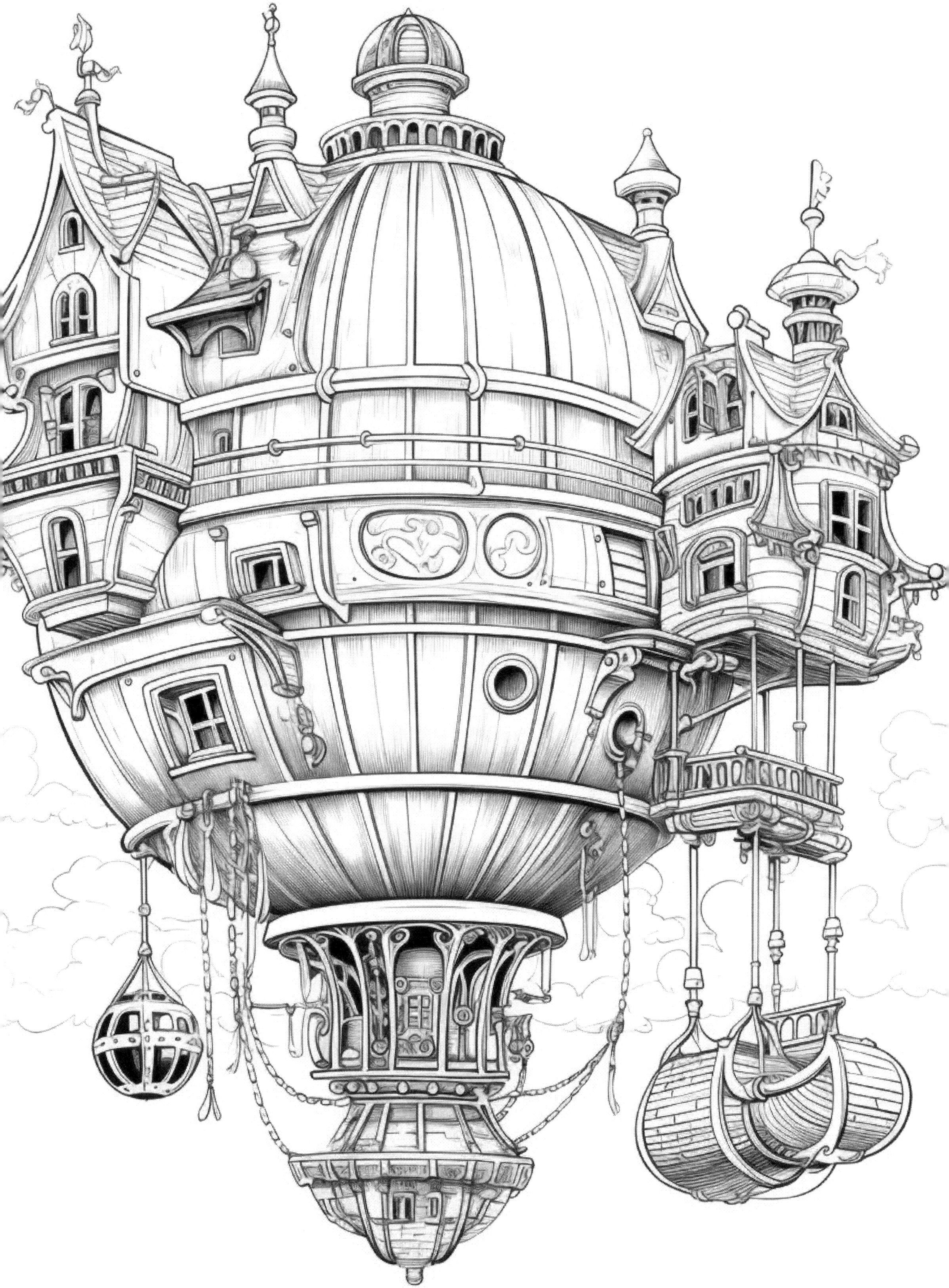

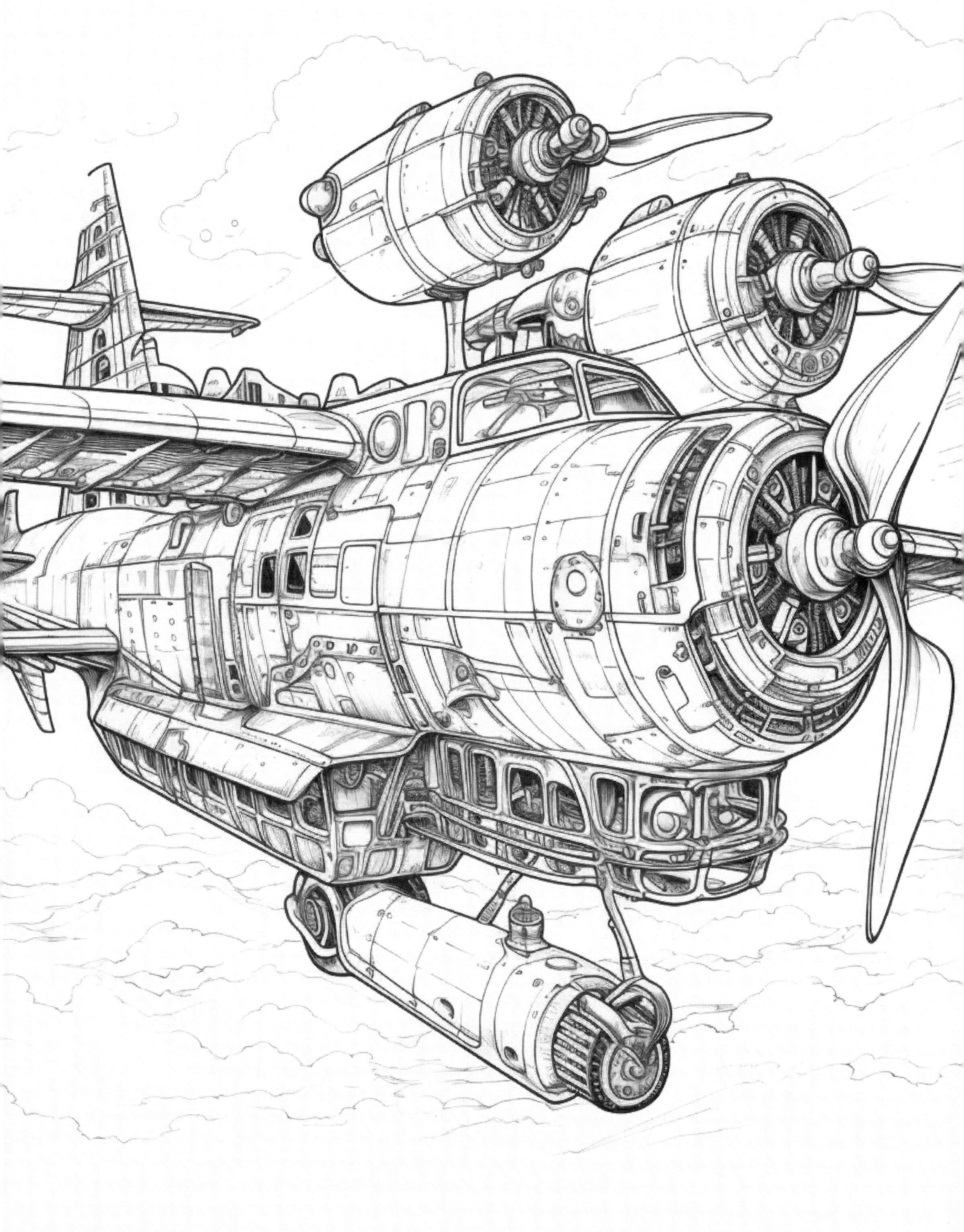

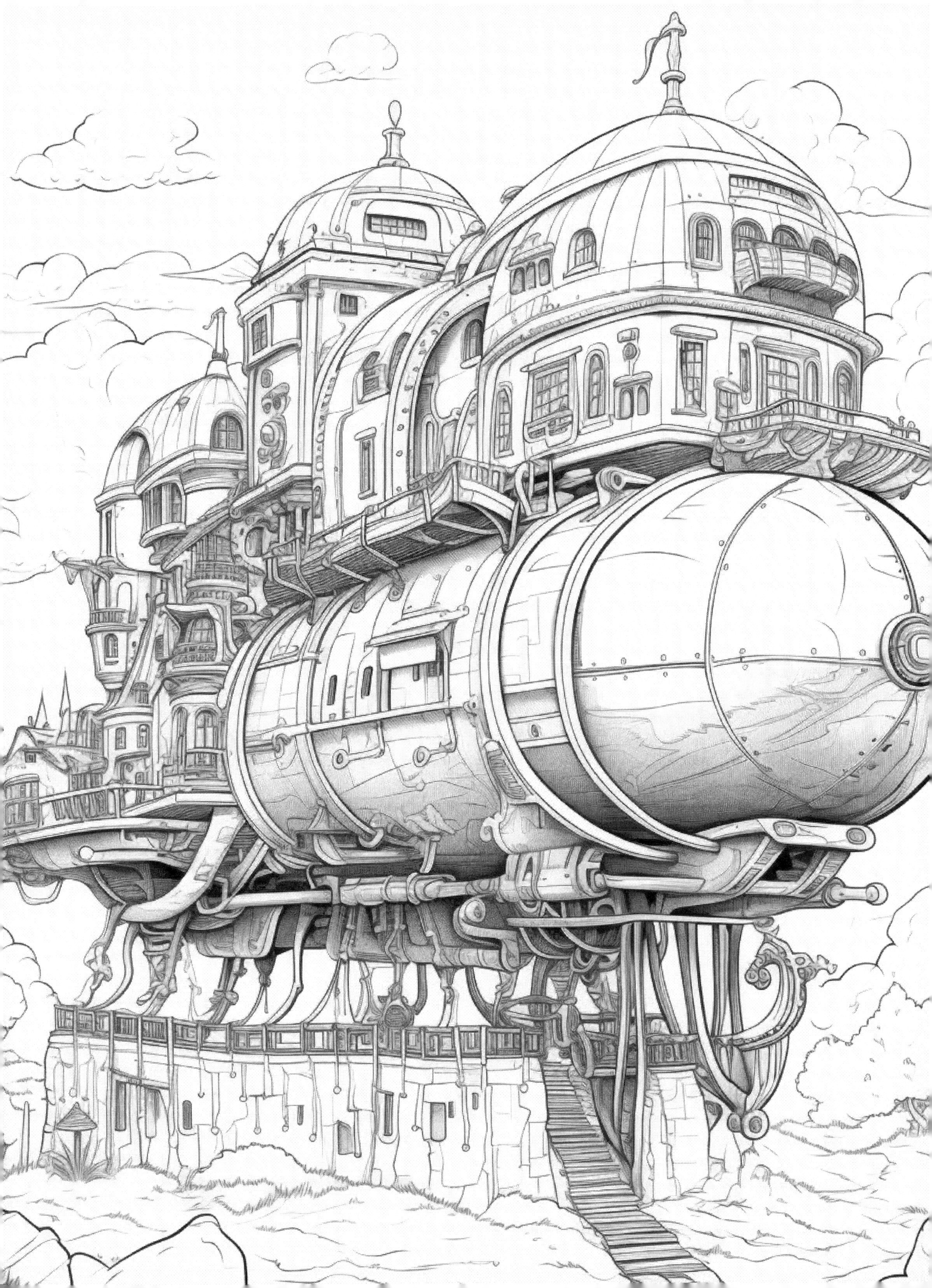

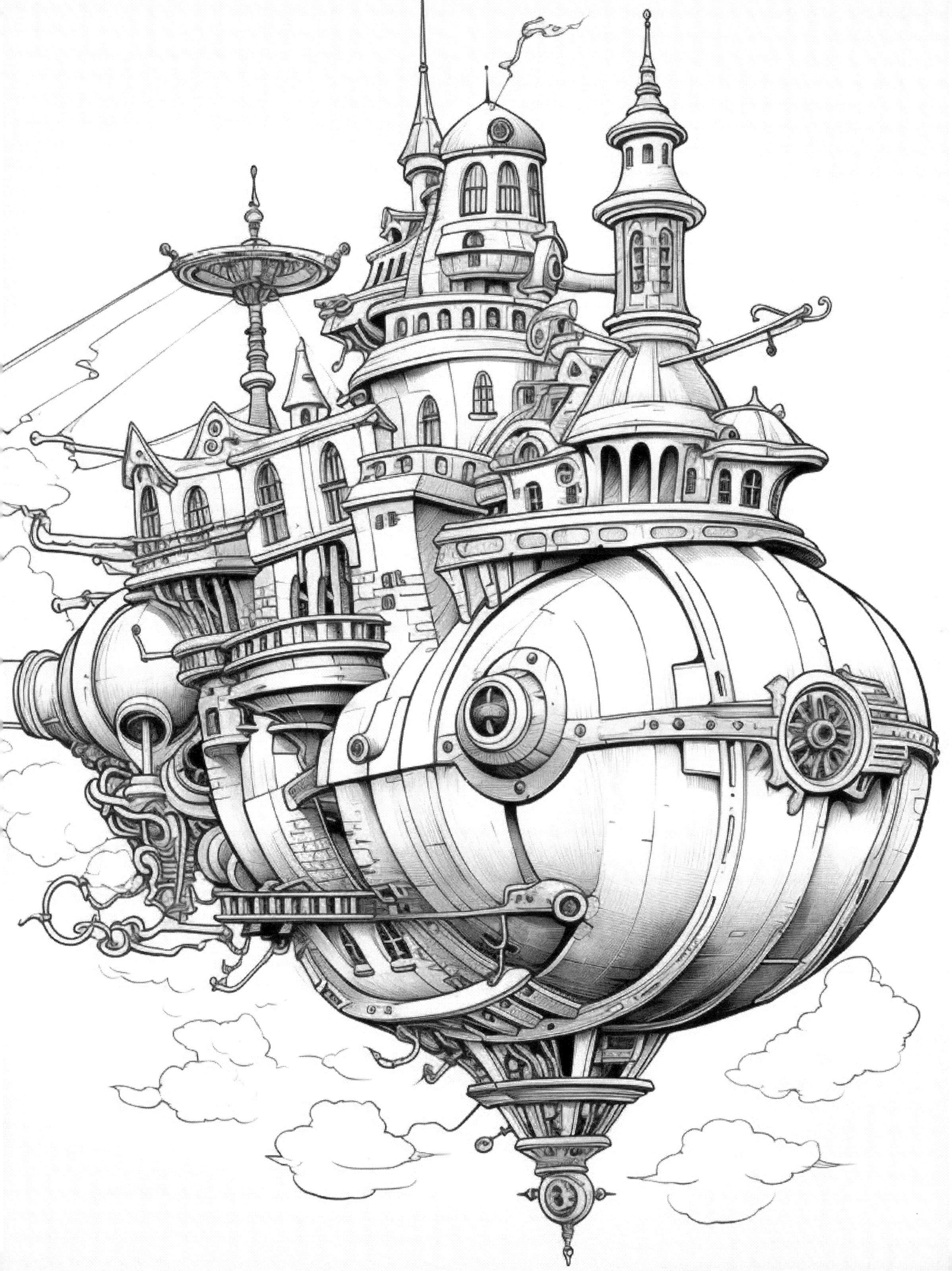

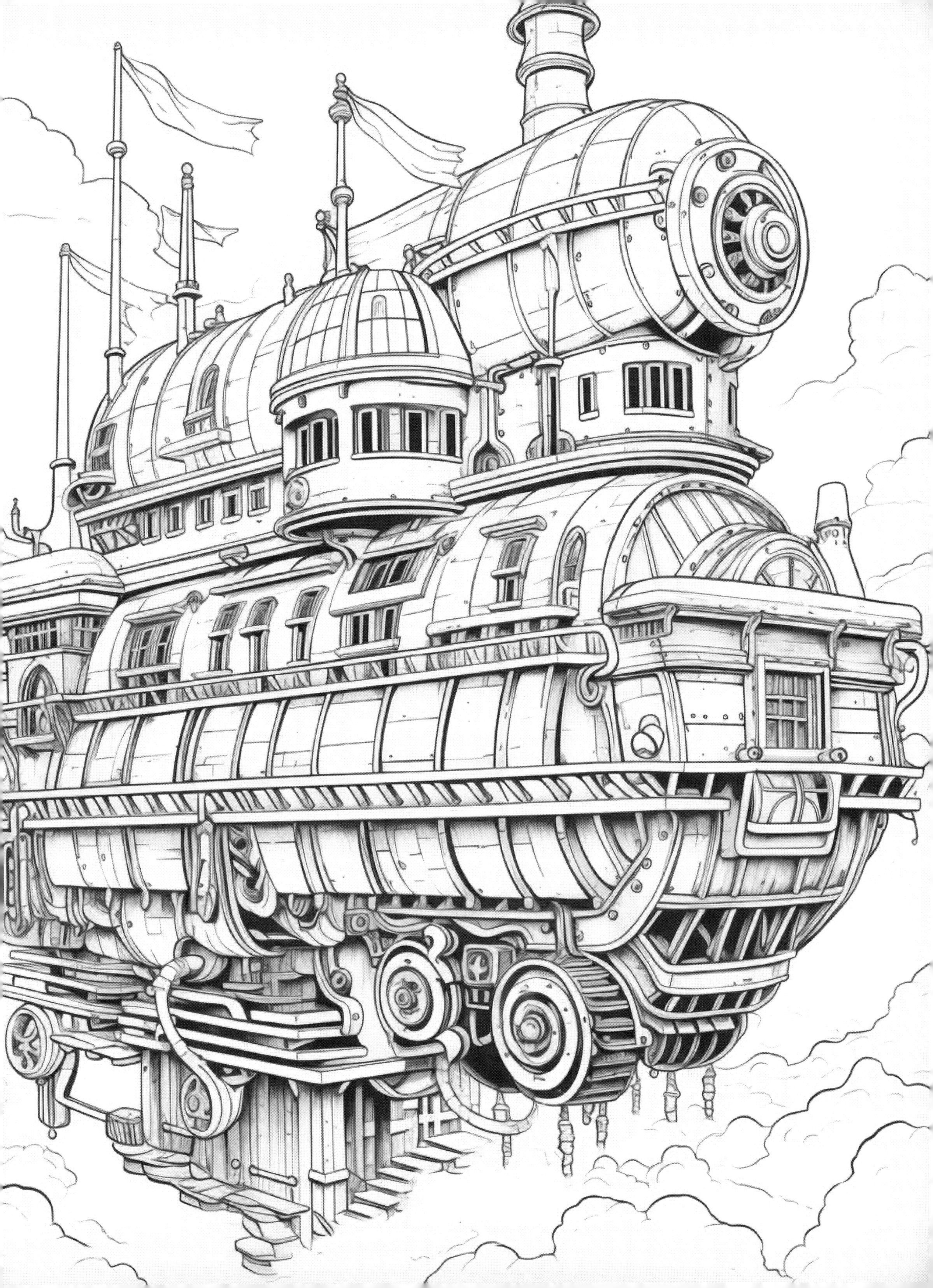

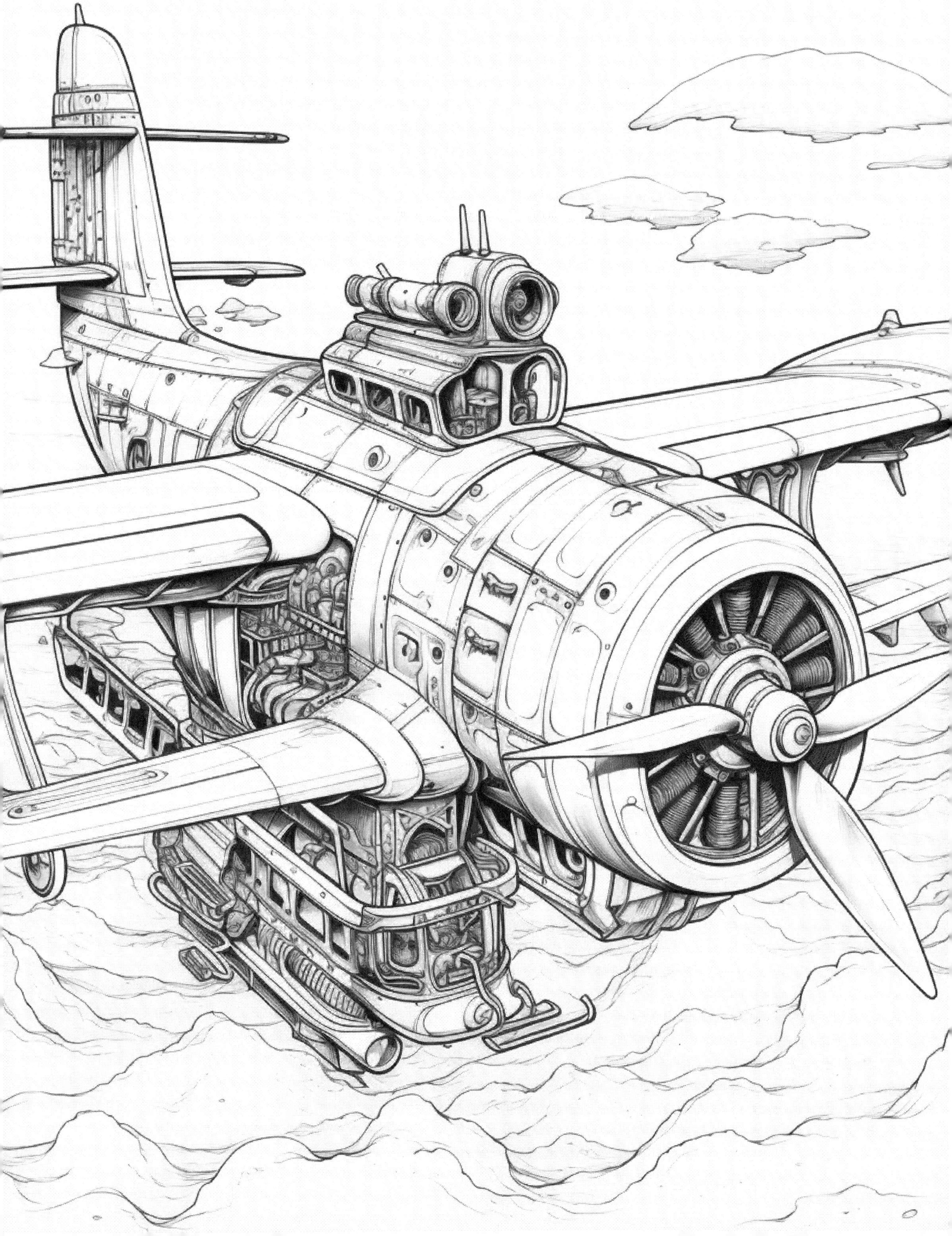

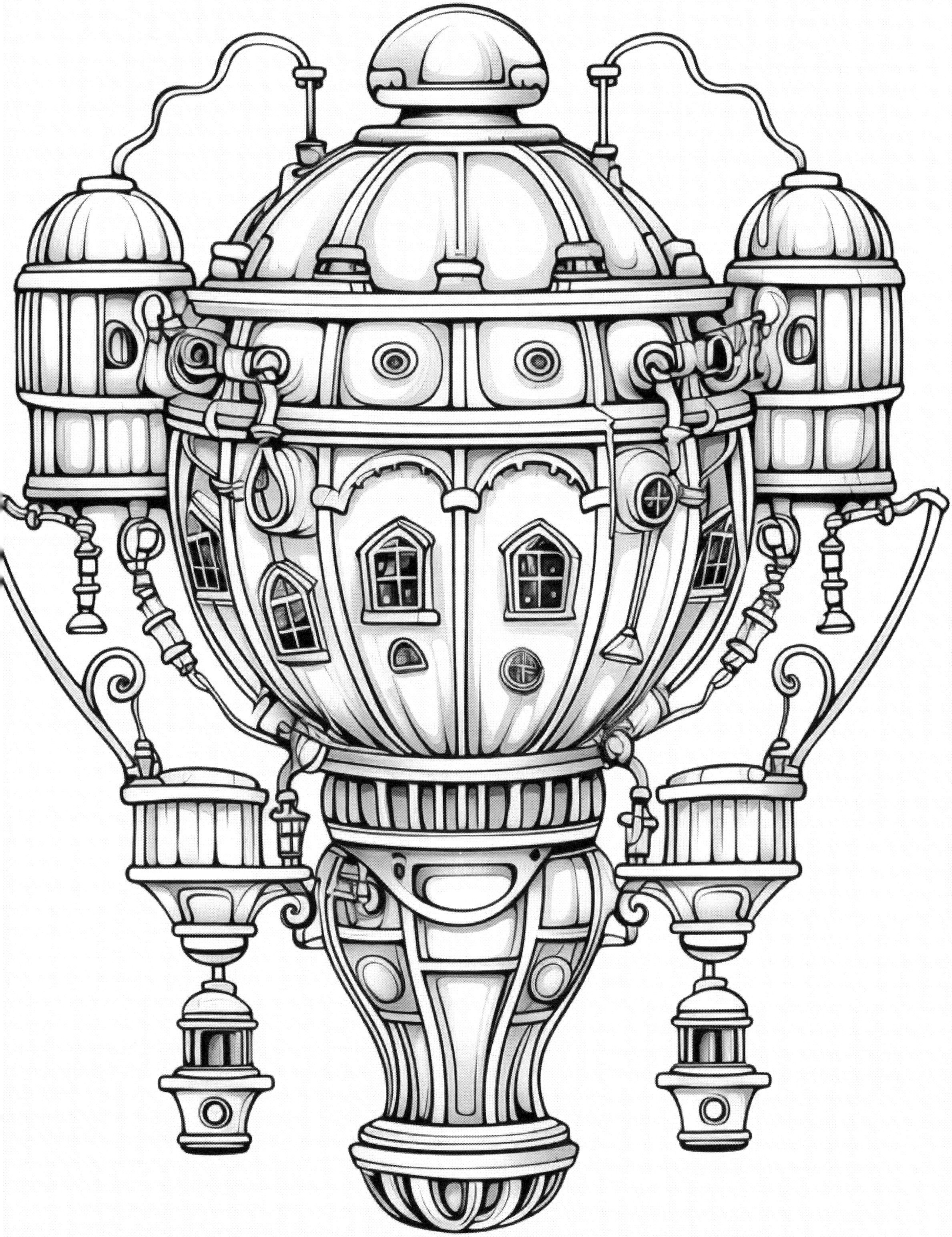

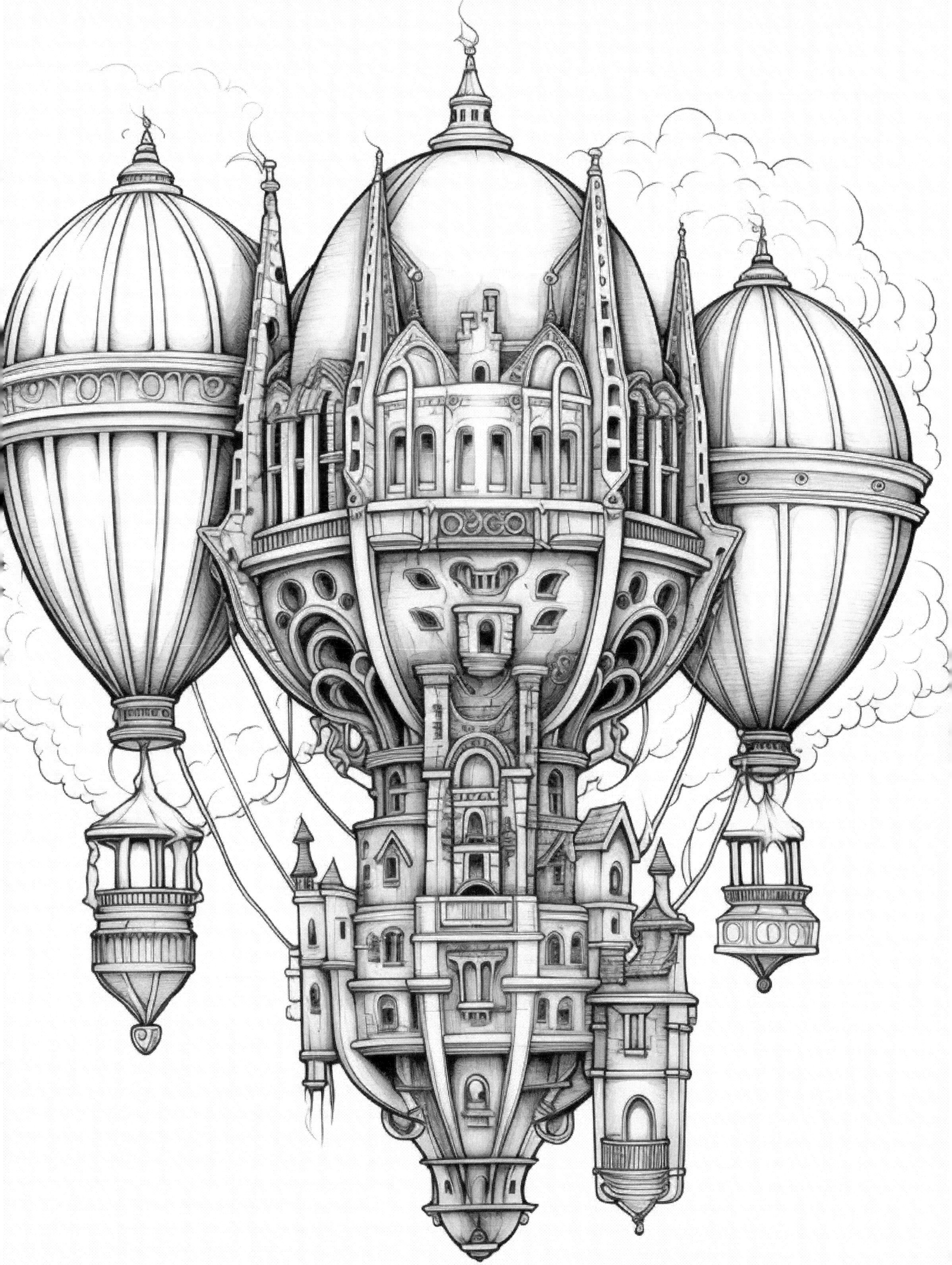

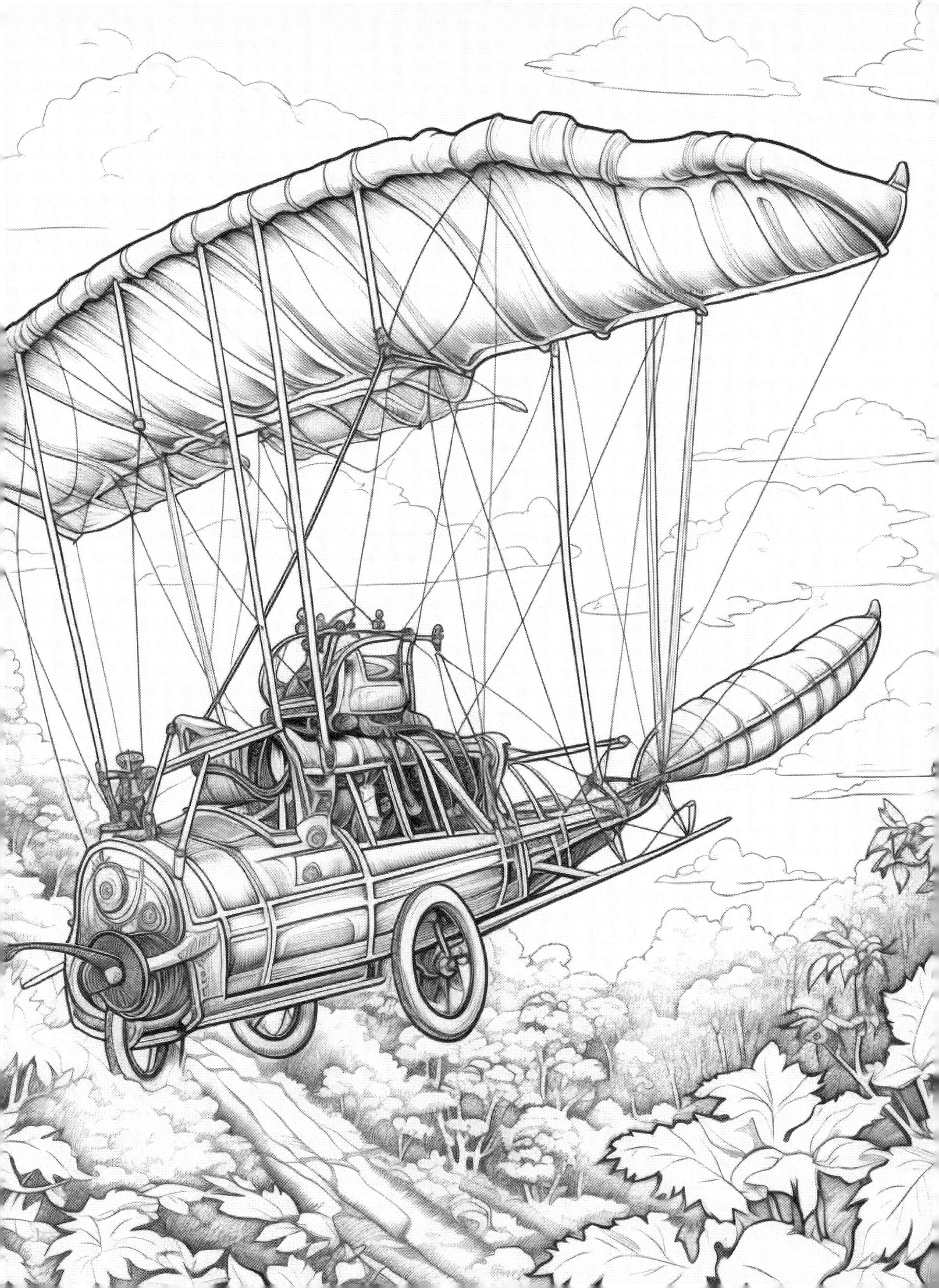

Made in the USA
Monee, IL
12 September 2023

42546158R00035